Contents

Preface to the Old Testament Notes.............
Introduction to Ezekiel................................
Chapter One..
Chapter Two..
Chapter Three..
Chapter Four...
Chapter Five.. 18
Chapter Six.. 20
Chapter Seven.. 22
Chapter Eight... 25
Chapter Nine.. 28
Chapter Ten.. 29
Chapter Eleven... 32
Chapter Twelve.. 35
Chapter Thirteen... 37
Chapter Fourteen.. 40
Chapter Fifteen... 42
Chapter Sixteen.. 42
Chapter Seventeen.. 50
Chapter Eighteen.. 53
Chapter Nineteen.. 55
Chapter Twenty.. 57
Chapter Twenty-One.. 62
Chapter Twenty-Two... 66
Chapter Twenty-Three... 69
Chapter Twenty-Four... 73
Chapter Twenty-Five... 77
Chapter Twenty-Six... 78
Chapter Twenty-Seven.. 80
Chapter Twenty-Eight... 85
Chapter Twenty-Nine.. 87
Chapter Thirty... 90
Chapter Thirty-One... 93
Chapter Thirty-Two.. 95
Chapter Thirty-Three.. 100
Chapter Thirty-Four... 102
Chapter Thirty-Five... 104
Chapter Thirty-Six... 105
Chapter Thirty-Seven.. 108
Chapter Thirty-Eight... 111
Chapter Thirty-Nine.. 114
Chapter Forty.. 117
Chapter Forty-One.. 122
Chapter Forty-Two... 125
Chapter Forty-Three... 127
Chapter Forty-Four... 130
Chapter Forty-Five... 134
Chapter Forty-Six... 137

Chapter Forty-Seven.. 138
Chapter Forty-Eight.. 140

Preface to the Old Testament Notes

1. ABOUT ten years ago I was prevailed upon to publish Explanatory Notes upon the New Testament. When that work was begun, and indeed when it was finished, I had no design to attempt any thing farther of the kind. Nay, I had a full determination, Not to do it, being throughly fatigued with the immense labour (had it been only this; tho' this indeed was but a small part of it,) of writing twice over a Quarto book containing seven or eight hundred pages.

2. But this was scarce published before I was importuned to write Explanatory Notes upon the Old Testament. This importunity I have withstood for many years. Over and above the deep conviction I had, of my insufficiency for such a work, of my want of learning, of understanding, of spiritual experience, for an undertaking more difficult by many degrees, than even writing on the New Testament, I objected, That there were many passages in the Old, which I did not understand myself, and consequently could not explain to others, either to their satisfaction, or my own. Above all, I objected the want of time: Not only as I have a thousand other employments, but as my Day is near spent, as I am declined into the vale of years. And to this day it appears to me as a dream, a thing almost incredible, that I should be entering upon a work of this kind, when I am entering into the sixty - third year of my age.

3. Indeed these considerations, the last particular, still appear to me of such weight, that I cannot entertain a thought of composing a body of Notes on the whole Old Testament. All the question remaining was, "Is there extant any Exposition which is worth abridging" Abundantly less time will suffice for this and less abilities of every kind. In considering this question, I soon turned my thought on the well - known Mr. Henry. He is allowed by all competent judges, to have been a person of strong understanding, of various learning, of solid piety, and much experience in the ways of God. And his exposition is generally clear and intelligible, the thoughts being expressed in plain words: It is also found, agreeable to the tenor of scripture, and to the analogy of faith. It is frequently full, giving a sufficient explication of the passages which require explaining. It is in many parts deep, penetrating farther into the inspired writings than most other comments do. It does not entertain us with vain speculations, but is practical throughout: and usually spiritual too teaching us how to worship God, not in form only, but in spirit and in truth.

4. But it may be reasonably enquired, "If Mr. Henry's exposition be not only plain, sound, full, and deep, but practical, yea and spiritual too, what need is there of any other Or how is it possible to mend This to alter it for the better" I answer, very many who have This, have no need of any other: particularly those who believe (what runs thro' the whole work and will much recommend it to them) the doctrine of absolution, irrespective, unconditional Predestination. I do not advise these, much to trouble themselves about any other exposition than Mr. Henry's: this is sufficient, thro' the assistance of the Blessed Spirit, to make private Christians wise unto salvation, and (the Lord applying his word) throughly furnished unto every good work.

5. But then it is manifest on the other hand, every one cannot have this exposition. It is too large a purchase: there are thousands who would rejoice

to have it; but it bears too high a price. They have not Six Guineas (the London price) in the world, perhaps from one year's end to another. And if they sometimes have, yet they have it not to spare; they need it for other occasions. How much soever therefore they desire so valuable a work, they must content themselves to go without it.

6. But suppose they have money enough to purchase, yet they have not time enough to read it: the size is as unsurmountable an objection as the price itself. It is not possible for men who have their daily bread to earn by the sweat of their brows, who generally are confined to their work, from six in the morning 'till six in the evening, to find leisure for reading over six folios, each containing seven or eight hundred pages. These therefore have need of some other exposition than Mr. Henry's. As excellent as it is in its kind, it is not for their purpose; seeing they have neither money to make the purchase, nor time to read it over.

7. It is very possible then to mend this work valuable as it is, at least by shortening it. As the grand objection to it is the size, that objection may be removed: and they who at present have no possibility of profiting by it, while it is of so great a bulk and so high a price, may then enjoy part at least of the same advantage with those who have more money and more leisure. Few I presume that have the whole and leisure to read it, will concern themselves with an extract. But those who cannot have all, will (for the present at least) be glad to have a part. And they who complain it is too short, may yet serve themselves of it, 'till they can procure the long work.

8. But I apprehend this valuable work may be made more valuable still, by making it plainer as well as shorter. Accordingly what is here extracted from it, (which indeed makes but a small part of the following volumes) is considerably plainer than the original. In order to this not only all the Latin sentences occasionally interspersed are omitted, but whatever phrases or words are not so intelligible to persons of no education. Those only who frequently and familiarly converse with men that are wholly uneducated, can conceive how many expressions are mere Greek to them, which are quite natural to those who have any share of learning. It is not by reading, much less by musing alone, that we are enabled to suit our discourse to common capacities. It is only by actually talking with the vulgar, that we learn to talk in a manner they can understand. And unless we do this, what do we profit them Do we not lose all our labour Should we speak as angels, we should be of no more use to them, than sounding brass or a tinkling cymbal.

9. Nay I apprehend what is extracted from Mr. Henry's work, may in some sense be more sound than the original. Understand me right: I mean more conformable to that glorious declaration, God willeth all men to be saved, and to come to the knowledge of his truth. And let it not be objected, That the making any alteration with regard to a point of doctrine, is a misrepresentation of the author's sense, and consequently an injury done to him. It would so, is an alteration were made of his words, so as to make them bear a different meaning; or if any words were recited as His, which he did not write. But neither of these is the case. Nothing is recited here as written by him which he did not write. Neither is any construction put upon his words, different from his own. But what he wrote in favour of Particular Redemption, is totally left out. And of

this I here give express notice to the reader once for all.

10. Again. It certainly possible that a work abundantly shorter than Mr. Henry's may nevertheless be considerably fuller, in some particulars. There are many words which he passes over without any explanation at all; as taking it for granted that the reader already knows the meaning of them. But this is a supposition not to be made; it is an entire mistake. For instance: What does a common man know of an Omer, or a Hin "Why Moses explains his own meaning: "An Omer is the tenth part of an Ephah." True; but what does the honest man know of an Ephah Just as much as of an Omer. I suppose that which led Mr. Henry into these omissions, which otherwise are unaccountable, was the desire of not saying what others had said before, Mr. Pool in particular. This is easily gathered from his own words, "Mr. Pool's English Annotations are of admirable use; especially for "the explaining of scripture phrases, opening the sense and clearing "of difficulties. I have industriously declined as much as I could what "is to be found there." I wish he had not. Or at least that he had given us the same sense in other words. Indeed he adds, "Those "and other annotations are most easy to be consulted upon occasion." Yes by those that have them: but that is not the case with the generality of Mr. Henry's readers. And besides they may justly expect that so large a comment will leave them no occasion to consult others.

11. It is possible likewise to penetrate deeper into the meaning of some scriptures than Mr. Henry has done. Altho' in general he is far from being a superficial writer, yet he is not always the same. Indeed if he had, he must have been more than man, considering the vastness of his work. It was scarce possible for any human understanding, to furnish out such a number of folios, without sinking sometimes into trite reflections and observations, rather lively than deep. A stream that runs wide and covers a large tract of land, will be shallow in some places. If it had been confined within a moderate channel, it might have flowed deep all along.

12. Nay, it cannot be denied, that there may be an exposition of scripture more closely practical, than some parts of Mr. Henry's are, as well as more spiritual. Even his exposition of the twentieth chapter of Exodus, where one would naturally have expected to find a compleat scheme of Christian practice, does not answer that expectation. Nor do I remember that he has any where given us, a satisfactory account of Spiritual Religion, of the kingdom of God within us, the fruit of Christ dwelling and reigning in the heart. This I hoped to have found particularly in the exposition of our Lord's Sermon upon the mount. But I was quite disappointed of my hope. It was not by any means what I expected.

13. I do not therefore intend the following Notes for a bare abridgment of Mr. Henry's exposition. Far from it: I not only omit much more than nineteen parts out of twenty of what he has written, but make many alterations and many additions, well nigh from the beginning to the end. In particular, I every where omit the far greater part of his inferences from and improvement of the chapter. They who think these the most valuable part of the work, may have recourse to the author himself. I likewise omit great part of almost every note, the sum of which is retained: as it seems to be his aim, to say as much, whereas it is mine to say as little as possible. And I omit

abundance of quaint sayings and lively antitheses; as, "God feeds his birds. Shall he not feed his babes!" "Pharaoh's princes: his pimps rather." Indeed every thing of this kind which occurred I have left quite untouched: altho' I am sensible these are the very flowers which numberless readers admire; nay which many, I doubt not, apprehend to be the chief beauties of the book. For that very reason I cannot but wish, they had never had a place therein; for this is a blemish, which is exceeding catching: he that admires it, will quickly imitate it. I used once to wonder, whence some whom I greatly esteem, had so many pretty turns in preaching. But when I read Mr. Henry, my wonder ceased. I saw, they were only copying after him: altho' many of them probably without designing or even adverting to it. They generally consulted his exposition of their text, and frequently just before preaching. And hence little witticisms and a kind of archness insensibly stole upon them, and took place of that strong, manly eloquence, which they would otherwise have learned from the inspired writers.

14. With regard to alterations, in what I take from Mr. Henry, I continually alter hard words into easy, and long sentences into short. But I do not knowingly alter the sense of any thing I extract from him, I only endeavour in several places, to make it more clear and determinate. I have here and there taken the liberty of altering a word in the text. But this I have done very sparingly, being afraid of venturing too far; as being conscious of my very imperfect acquaintance with the Hebrew tongue. I have added very largely from Mr. Pool, as much as seemed necessary for common readers, in order to their understanding those words or passages, which Mr. Henry does not explain. Nay, from the time that I had more maturely considered Mr. Pool's annotations on the Bible, (which was soon after I had gone thro' the book of Genesis) I have extracted far more from him than from Mr. Henry: it having been my constant method, after reading the text, first to read and weigh what Mr. Pool observed upon every verse, and afterwards to consult Mr. Henry's exposition of the whole paragraph. In consequence of this, instead of short additions from Mr. Pool to supply what was wanting in Mr. Henry, (which was my first design) I now only make extracts from Mr. Henry, to supply so far as they are capable, what was wanting in Mr. Pool. I say, so far as they are capable: for I still found in needful to add to both such farther observations, as have from time to time occurred to my own mind in reading or thinking on the scriptures, together with such as I have occasionally extracted from other authors.

15. Every thinking man will now easily discern my design in the following sheets. It is not, to write sermons, essays or set discourses, upon any part of scripture. It is not to draw inferences from the text, or to shew what doctrines may be proved thereby. It is this: To give the direct, literal meaning, of every verse, of every sentence, and as far as I am able, of every word in the oracles of God. I design only, like the hand of a dial, to point every man to This: not to take up his mind with something else, how excellent soever: but to keep his eye fixt upon the naked Bible, that he may read and hear it with understanding. I say again, (and desire it may be well observed, that none may expect what they will not find) It is not my design to write a book, which a man may read separate from the Bible: but barely to assist those who fear God, in hearing and reading the bible itself, by shewing the natural sense of every part, in as few and plain words as I can.

16. And I am not without hopes, that the following notes may in some measure answer this end, not barely to unlettered and ignorant men, but also to men of education and, learning: (altho' it is true, neither these nor the Notes on the New Testament were principally designed for Them.) Sure I am, that tracts wrote in the most plain and simple manner, are of infinitely more service to me, than those which are elaborated with the utmost skill, and set off with the greatest pomp of erudition.

17. But it is no part of my design, to save either learned or unlearned men from the trouble of thinking. If so, I might perhaps write Folios too, which usually overlay, rather than help the thought. On the contrary, my intention is, to make them think, and assist them in thinking. This is the way to understand the things of God; Meditate thereon day and night; So shall you attain the best knowledge; even to know the only true God and Jesus Christ whom He hath sent. And this knowledge will lead you, to love Him, because he hath first loved us: yea, to love the Lord your God with all your heart, and with all your soul, and with all your mind, and with all your strength. Will there not then be all that mind in you, which was also in Christ Jesus And in consequence of this, while you joyfully experience all the holy tempers described in this book, you will likewise be outwardly holy as He that hath called you is holy, in all manner of conversation.

18. If you desire to read the scripture in such a manner as may most effectually answer this end, would it not be advisable, 1. To set apart a little time, if you can, every morning and evening for that purpose 2. At each time if you have leisure, to read a chapter out of the Old, and one out of the New Testament: is you cannot do this, to take a single chapter, or a part of one 3. To read this with a single eye, to know the whole will of God, and a fixt resolution to do it In order to know his will, you should, 4. Have a constant eye to the analogy of faith; the connexion and harmony there is between those grand, fundamental doctrines, Original Sin, Justification by Faith, the New Birth, Inward and Outward Holiness. 5. Serious and earnest prayer should be constantly used, before we consult the oracles of God, seeing "scripture can only be understood thro' the same Spirit whereby "it was given." Our reading should likewise be closed with prayer, that what we read may be written on our hearts. 6. It might also be of use, if while we read, we were frequently to pause, and examine ourselves by what we read, both with regard to our hearts, and lives. This would furnish us with matter of praise, where we found God had enabled us to conform to his blessed will, and matter of humiliation and prayer, where we were conscious of having fallen short. And whatever light you then receive, should be used to the uttermost, and that immediately. Let there be no delay. Whatever you resolve, begin to execute the first moment you can. So shall you find this word to be indeed the power of God unto present and eternal salvation.

EDINBURGH,

April 25, 1765.

Introduction to Ezekiel

The name Ezekiel signifies, The strength of God. And God did indeed make his face strong against all opposition. It was the tradition of the Jews, that for his boldness and faithfulness in reproving them, he was put to death by the captives in Babylon.

The prophecies of this book were spoken and written in Babylon, to the Jews who were captives there. Ezekiel prophesied in the beginning of their captivity, to convince them when they were secure and unhumbled; Daniel, in the latter end of it, to comfort them, when they were dejected and discouraged.

There is much in this book which is very mysterious, especially in the beginning and latter end of it. But tho' the visions are intricate, the sermons are plain, and the design of them is, to shew God's people their transgressions. And tho' the reproofs and threatenings are very sharp, yet toward the close we have very comfortable promises, to be fulfilled in the kingdom of the Messiah, of whom indeed Ezekiel speaks less than almost any of the prophets.

The visions, which are his credentials, we have, chap. 1 - 3. The reproofs and threatenings, chap. 4 - 24. We have messages sent to the neighbouring nations, foretelling their destruction, chap. 25 - 35. To make way for the restoration of Israel, and the re-establishment of their city and temple, which are foretold, chap. 36 – 48.

Chapter One

The time when this prophecy was delivered, the place where, and person by whom, ver. 1 - 3.
His vision of the glory of God, in his attendance, surrounded with angels, (here called living creatures) ver. 4 - 14.
In his providences, represented by the wheels and their motions, ver. 15 - 26. And in the face of Jesus Christ, sitting upon the throne, ver. 26 - 28.

Verse 1

1 Now it came to pass in the thirtieth year, in the fourth month, in the fifth day of the month, as I was among the captives by the river of Chebar, that the heavens were opened, and I saw visions of God.

Thirtieth year — From the finding the book of the law in the eighteenth year of Josiah, from which date to the fifth year of the captivity are thirty years.

Fifth day — Probably it was the sabbath-day, when the Jews were at leisure to hear the prophet.

River — Perhaps retiring thither to lament their own sins, and Jerusalem's desolation.

Chebar — A river now called Giulap, arising out of the mountain Masius, and falling into Euphrates, somewhat below a city called by the same name.

Verse 2

2 In the fifth day of the month, which was the fifth year of king Jehoiachin's captivity,

The month — Thamus, as verse 1, answering to our June and July.

Fifth year — This account observed will guide us in computing the times referred to verse 1. These five of Jehoiachin, and the eleven of his predecessor, added to fourteen of Josiah's reign, after he found the law, make up thirty years, verse 1.

Jehoiachin — Who is also called Jechoniah, and Coniah. It may be of use to keep an account, when and where God has manifested himself to us in a peculiar manner. Remember, O my soul, what thou didst receive at such a time, at such a place: tell others what God did for thee.

Verse 3

3 The word of the LORD came expressly unto Ezekiel the priest, the son of Buzi, in the land of the Chaldeans by the river Chebar; and the hand of the LORD was there upon him.

The word — What was visions, verse 1, is here the word, both as signifying and declaring the mind of God, what he would do, and as continuing his commands to Ezekiel and to the people.

Ezekiel — He speaks of himself in a third person.

Priest — He was of the priests originally; he was a prophet by an extraordinary call.

The hand — He felt the power of God opening his eyes to see the visions, opening his ear to hear the voice, and his heart to receive both. When the hand of the Lord goes along with his word, then it becomes effectual.

Verse 4

4 And I looked, and, behold, a whirlwind came out of the north, a great cloud, and a fire infolding itself, and a brightness was about it, and out of the midst thereof as the colour of amber, out of the midst of the fire.

Looked — I very diligently surveyed the things that were represented to me in the vision.

Whirlwind — This denotes the indignation and judgments of God; a quick, impetuous and irresistible vengeance.

North — From Babylon, which lay northward from Judea; and the prophet, tho' now in Babylon, speaks of the Jews, as if they were in Jerusalem.

A fire — An orb or wheel of fire: God being his own cause, his own rule, and his own end.

Brightness — Yet round about it was not smoak and darkness, but a clear light.

The midst — Of the fire.

Verse 5

5 Also out of the midst thereof came the likeness of four living creatures. And this was their appearance; they had the likeness of a man.

The likeness — Such a representation of the holy angels as God saw fit to make use of, came out of the midst of the fire: for angels derive their being and power from God: their glory is a ray of his.

Verse 6

6 And every one had four faces, and every one had four wings.

Wings — With two they flew, denoting the speed of their obedience; and with two they covered their body, denoting their reverence.

Verse 7

7 And their feet were straight feet; and the sole of their feet was like the sole of a calf's foot: and they sparkled like the colour of burnished brass.

Feet — Their thighs, legs and feet, were of a human shape.

Straight — Not bowed to this or that part, which argues weakness.

The sole — That which is properly the foot.

A calf's — A divided hoof spake the cleanness of the creature.

They — Their feet.

Verse 8

8 And they had the hands of a man under their wings on their four sides; and they four had their faces and their wings.

Under — Their power and manner of exerting it is secret and invisible.

Sides — On each side of the chariot one of these living creatures flood, and so on each side hands were ready to act as they were moved.

They four — It is doubled to confirm the truth and certainty of the thing.

Verse 9

9 Their wings were joined one to another; they turned not when they went; they went every one straight forward.

Their wings — The wings of the two cherubim which went foremost, and the wings of the two hindermost, were joined together when they moved.

Went — This explains the former words, assuring us, that every one of those living creatures are ready, and unwearied in doing the pleasure of their Creator.

Verse 10

10 As for the likeness of their faces, they four had the face of a man, and the face of a lion, on the right side: and they four had the face of an ox on the left side; they four also had the face of an eagle.

A man — Each face is compared to what is most excellent in its kind, man excels in wisdom, lions in strength, the ox in patience and constancy of labour, the eagle in speed and high flight.

Verse 11

11 Thus were their faces: and their wings were stretched upward; two wings of every one were joined one to another, and two covered their bodies.

Divided — So each face appeared distinct above the shoulders, and there the wings divided from each other were united to the body of the living creature.

Verse 12

12 And they went every one straight forward: whither the spirit was to go, they went; and they turned not when they went.

Straight — Which way soever they went, each living creature had one face looking straight forward.

The spirit — The will, command, and breathing of the Spirit of God, both gave and guided their motions.

Was to go — Going is attributed here

to the Spirit of God, by allusion, for he who is in every place cannot properly be said to go from or to any place.

Turned not — They looked not back, they turned not out of the way, they gave not over, 'till they had compleated their course.

Verse 13

13 As for the likeness of the living creatures, their appearance was like burning coals of fire, and like the appearance of lamps: it went up and down among the living creatures; and the fire was bright, and out of the fire went forth lightning.

The fire — This fire stood not still, but as the Hebrew is, Made itself walk up and down. It moved itself, which is too much to ascribe to creatures: God only moved all these living creatures.

Verse 14

14 And the living creatures ran and returned as the appearance of a flash of lightning.

Ran — They ran into the lower world, to do what was to be done there: and when they had done, returned as a flash of lightning, to the upper world, to the vision of God. Thus we should be in the affairs of this world: though we run into them we must not repose in them, but our souls must presently return like lightning, to God, their rest and center.

Verse 15

15 Now as I beheld the living creatures, behold one wheel upon the earth by the living creatures, with his four faces.

Living creatures — By each of the living creatures stood one wheel, so that they were four in number, according to the number of living creatures.

Four faces — By this it appears, each wheel had its four faces. While he was contemplating the glory of the former vision, this other was presented to him: wherein the dispensations of providence are compared to the wheels of a machine, which all contribute to the regular motion of it. Providence orders, changes: sometimes one spoke of the wheel is uppermost, sometimes another. But the motion of the wheel on its own axle-tree, is still regular and steady. And the wheel is said to be by the living creatures, who attend to direct its motion. For all inferior creatures are, and move, and act, as the Creator, by the ministration of angels directs and influences them: visible effects are managed and governed by invisible causes.

Verse 16

16 The appearance of the wheels and their work was like unto the colour of a beryl: and they four had one likeness: and their appearance and their work was as it were a wheel in the middle of a wheel.

Work — All that was wrought, whether engraved or otherwise was of one colour.

Beryl — A sea green.

One likeness — The same for dimensions, colour, frame, and motion.

In the middle — It is probable, the wheels were framed so as to be an exact sphere, which is easily rolled to any side.

Verse 17

17 When they went, they went upon their four sides: and they turned not when they went.

They — The wheels.

Four sides — The wheels being supposed round every way as a globe, by an exact framing of two wheels one in the other; the four semi-circles which are in two whole wheels, may be well taken for these four sides on which these wheels move, and such a wheel will readily be turned to all points of the compass.

Returned not — They returned not 'till they came to their journey's end; nothing could divert them, or put them out of their course. So firm and sure are the methods, so unalterable and constant the purposes of God, and so invariable the obedience and observance of holy angels. So subject to the sovereign will of God are all second causes.

Verse 18

18 As for their rings, they were so high that they were dreadful; and their rings were full of eyes round about them four.

The rings — The circumference of the wheels.

Dreadful — Their very height imprest a fear on the beholder.

Them four — Every one of the four wheels. How fitly do the wheels, their motion, their height, and eyes, signify the height, unsearchableness, wisdom, and vigilance of the Divine Providence.

Verse 20

20 Whithersoever the spirit was to go, they went, thither was their spirit to go; and the wheels were lifted up over against them: for the spirit of the living creature was in the wheels.

The spirit — The Spirit of God. These angels in their ministry punctually observed both his impulse and conduct.

They — The wheels, inferior agents and second causes.

Their spirit — The wheels concurred with the spirit of the living creatures, so that there was an hearty accord between those superior and inferior causes.

For — An undiscerned, yet divine, mighty, wise, and ever-living power, spirit, and being, actuated all, and governed all.

Verse 21

21 When those went, these went; and when those stood, these stood; and when those were lifted up from the earth, the wheels were lifted up over against them: for the spirit of the living creatures was in the wheels.

For — The same wisdom, power, and holiness of God, the same will and counsel of his, that guides and governs the angels, does by them order and dispose all the motions of the creatures in this lower world.

Verse 22

22 And the likeness of the firmament upon the heads of the living creature was as the colour of the terrible crystal, stretched forth over their heads above.

Likeness — The appearance or resemblance.

As crystal — For splendor, purity, and solidity, all that was above these creatures and wheels was beautiful and very majestic, and 'tis therefore called terrible, because it impressed a veneration upon the mind of the beholders.

Verse 23

23 And under the firmament were their wings straight, the one toward the other: every one had two, which covered on this side, and every one had two, which covered on that side, their bodies.

Under — Below at a great distance, stood these living creatures.

Straight — Stretched forth, ready for motion.

One — Each of the four had two other wings with which they covered their bodies.

Verse 24

24 And when they went, I heard the noise of their wings, like the noise of great waters, as the voice of the Almighty, the voice of speech, as the noise of an host: when they stood, they let down their wings.

The voice — Thunder.

Speech — The prophet heard the voice in an articulate manner.

An host — A tumultuous voice of men.

Stood — Having done their office they present themselves before God, waiting for the commands of their Lord.

Verse 26

26 And above the firmament that was over their heads was the likeness of a throne, as the appearance of a sapphire stone: and upon the likeness of the throne was the likeness as the appearance of a man above upon it.

A man — Christ, God-man, who here appears as king and judge.

Verse 27

27 And I saw as the colour of amber, as the appearance of fire round about within it, from the appearance of his loins even upward, and from the appearance of his loins even downward, I saw as it were the appearance of fire, and it had brightness round about.

Amber — In this colour does Christ appear against the rebellious Jews; he that would have visited them clothed with the garments of salvation, now puts on the garments of vengeance, expressed by such metaphors.

Brightness — Majesty, justice, and unstained holiness, shine round about him.

Verse 28

28 As the appearance of the bow that is in the cloud in the day of rain, so was the appearance of the brightness round about. This was the appearance of the likeness of the glory of the LORD. And when I saw it, I fell upon my face, and I heard a voice of one that spake.

The bow — A like appearance of Christ in a surrounding brightness, as of the rainbow you have, Revelation 4:3. Mercy, and truth, and both according to covenant are about the throne of Christ.

Glory — It was not the full glory of God, but such as the prophet might bear.

I fell — With deep humility and reverence.

Chapter Two

Ezekiel is commissioned to prophesy to the Jewish captives, ver. 1 - 5.
Is cautioned not to be afraid of them, ver. 6.
Has words put into his mouth, signified by the vision of a roll, which he is ordered to eat, ver. 7 - 10.

Verse 1

1 And he said unto me, Son of man, stand upon thy feet, and I will speak unto thee.

And — He that sat upon the throne, Jesus Christ.

Son of man — A phrase which is ninety-five times, at least, used in this prophecy to keep him humble who had such great revelations.

Stand — Arise, fear not. And with this command God sent forth a power enabling him to rise and stand.

Verse 2

2 And the spirit entered into me when he spake unto me, and set me upon my feet, that I heard him that spake unto me.

The spirit — The same spirit which actuated the living creatures.

Verse 5

5 And they, whether they will hear, or whether they will forbear, (for they are a rebellious house,) yet shall know that there hath been a prophet among them.

Shall know — They that obey shall know by the good I will do them, those that will not, by the evil which I will bring upon them.

Verse 6

6 And thou, son of man, be not afraid of them, neither be afraid of their words, though briers and thorns be with thee, and thou dost dwell among scorpions: be not afraid of their words, nor be dismayed at their looks, though they be a rebellious house.

Words — Accusations, threats, or whatever else a malicious heart can suggest to the tongue.

Briars — Which usually run up among thorns, are a very fit emblem of the frowardness and keenness of sinners against God and his prophet.

Scorpious — Malicious, revengeful men. They that will do any thing to purpose in the service of God, must not fear the faces of men.

Verse 8

8 But thou, son of man, hear what I say unto thee; Be not thou rebellious like that rebellious house: open thy mouth, and eat that I give thee.

Hear — Obey.

Open — This was done only in a vision.

Verse 9

9 And when I looked, behold, an hand was sent unto me; and, lo, a roll of a book was therein;

Roll — Their books were not like ours,

but written in parchment and in the length of it, and so one piece fastened to another, 'till the whole would contain what was to be written, and then it was wrapped or rolled about a round piece of wood, fashioned for that purpose.

Verse 10

10 And he spread it before me; and it was written within and without: and there was written therein lamentations, and mourning, and woe.

And — The person, who held out his hand.

Spread — Unrolled it.

Within ... — On both sides, on that side which was inward when rolled, and on that side also that was outward.

Chapter Three

His eating the roll, ver. 1 - 3.
Farther instructions and encouragements given him, ver. 4 - 11.
He is carried to the captive Jews, ver. 12 - 15.
An illustration of his office by that of a watchman, ver. 16 - 21.
The restraining and restoring of his liberty of speech, ver. 22 - 27.

Verse 1

1 Moreover he said unto me, Son of man, eat that thou findest; eat this roll, and go speak unto the house of Israel.

Eat — This was done in a vision.

Findeth — In the hand which was sent to him.

Verse 3

3 And he said unto me, Son of man, cause thy belly to eat, and fill thy bowels with this roll that I give thee. Then did I eat it; and it was in my mouth as honey for sweetness.

Belly — The mouth is the proper instrument of eating, but when meat is digested, the belly is said to eat.

Fill thy bowels — This denotes the fulness of the measure wherewith we should read, meditate, and digest the word of God.

Honey — It was sweet to receive things by revelation from God, and so to converse with God. And usually the first part of the ministerial work is pleasant.

Verse 4

4 And he said unto me, Son of man, go, get thee unto the house of Israel, and speak with my words unto them.

Speak — What things I shall shew thee, and in what words I shall declare them to thee.

Verse 6

6 Not to many people of a strange speech and of an hard language, whose words thou canst not understand. Surely, had I sent thee to them, they would have hearkened unto thee.

Many people — Divers nations, that thou shouldest need divers tongues, to speak to them all in their own language.

Verse 7

7 But the house of Israel will not hearken unto thee; for they will not hearken unto me: for all the house of Israel are impudent and hardhearted.

All — The far greater part, tho' not every particular person.

Verse 8

8 Behold, I have made thy face strong against their faces, and thy forehead strong against their foreheads.

I have — I have given thee, constancy, and manly carriage. The more impudent wicked people are in their opposition to religion, the more openly and resolutely should God's people appear in the practice and defence of it.

Verse 11

11 And go, get thee to them of the captivity, unto the children of thy people, and speak unto them, and tell them, Thus saith the Lord GOD; whether they will hear, or whether they will forbear.

Captivity — Of the first captivity under Jeconiah's reign, who succeeded his father Jehoiakim, slain for his conspiracy with Egypt against Nebuchadnezzar.

Verse 12

12 Then the spirit took me up, and I heard behind me a voice of a great rushing, saying, Blessed be the glory of the LORD from his place.

A voice — An articulate sound, of many angels, attended with the rushing of the wheels, added to the noise of their wings.

Blessed — Praised be the gloriously holy and just God.

His place — Coming down from heaven.

Verse 13

13 I heard also the noise of the wings of the living creatures that touched one another, and the noise of the wheels over against them, and a noise of a great rushing.

Rushing — The wheels of providence moved over against the angels, and in concert with them.

Verse 14

14 So the spirit lifted me up, and took me away, and I went in bitterness, in the heat of my spirit; but the hand of the LORD was strong upon me.

Spirit — Caught him up into the air.

Took — Carried me to the place where the captive Jews were crowded together.

Bitterness — Not at all pleased with my work. He went in the heat of his spirit; because of the discouragements he foresaw he should meet with. But the hand of the Lord was strong upon him, not only to compel him to the work, but to fit him for it.

Verse 15

15 Then I came to them of the captivity at Telabib, that dwelt by the river of Chebar, and I sat where they sat, and remained there astonished among them seven days.

Tel-abib — A part of Mesopotamia, which was shut up within Chebar westward, and Saocora eastward.

By — On that part of the river Chebar, which runs west-ward of Tel-abib.

Where — Where I found them sitting astonished, at the sight of their change from freedom and honour to servitude and shame.

Seven days — Mourning no doubt all that while, and waiting 'till the spirit of prophecy should open his mouth.

Verse 20

20 Again, When a righteous man doth turn from his righteousness, and commit iniquity, and I lay a stumblingblock before him, he shall die: because thou hast not given him warning, he shall die in his sin, and his righteousness which he hath done shall not be remembered; but his blood will I require at thine hand.

I Lay — Permit it to be laid before him.

He shall — Perish in his sin.

Remembered — Shall not be profitable to him; "he that apostatizes is the worst of men, because he falls from known ways of goodness and holiness."

Verse 22

22 And the hand of the LORD was there upon me; and he said unto me, Arise, go forth into the plain, and I will there talk with thee.

There — At Tel-abib.

Go forth — Withdraw from the multitude.

Verse 23

23 Then I arose, and went forth into the plain: and, behold, the glory of the LORD stood there, as the glory which I saw by the river of Chebar: and I fell on my face.

As the glory — We are not now to expect such visions. But we have a favour done us nothing inferior, if we by faith behold the glory of the Lord, so as to be changed into the same image. And this honour have all his saints.

Verse 24

24 Then the spirit entered into me, and set me upon my feet, and spake with me, and said unto me, Go, shut thyself within thine house.

Shut — To foresignify the shutting up of the Jews in Jerusalem.

Verse 25

25 But thou, O son of man, behold, they shall put bands upon thee, and shall bind thee with them, and thou shalt not go out among them:

Not go — Thou shalt be straitly confined.

Verse 26

26 And I will make thy tongue cleave to the roof of thy mouth, that thou shalt be dumb, and shalt not be to them a reprover: for they are a rebellious house.

I — I will make thee as dumb as if thy tongue clave to the roof of thy mouth.

Verse 27

27 But when I speak with thee, I will open thy mouth, and thou shalt say unto them, Thus saith the Lord GOD; He that heareth, let him hear; and he that forbeareth, let him forbear: for they are a rebellious house.

But — When ever I shall reveal any thing to thee.

Open — I will give thee power to speak.

Let — 'Tis his duty and safety.

Forbear — 'Tis at his own peril.

Chapter Four

Two things are here represented to the prophet in vision, The fortifications that shall be shortly raised against the city, signified by his laying siege to the portrait of Jerusalem, ver. 1 - 3.
And lying first on one side, and then on the other side before it, ver. 4 - 8.
The famine that would rage therein, signified by his eating coarse fare, and little of it, so long as this typical representation lasted, ver. 9 - 17.

Verse 1

1 Thou also, son of man, take thee a tile, and lay it before thee, and pourtray upon it the city, even Jerusalem:

Portray — Draw a map of Jerusalem.

Verse 2

2 And lay siege against it, and build a fort against it, and cast a mount against it; set the camp also against it, and set battering rams against it round about.

Lay siege — Draw the figure of a siege about the city.

Build — Raise a tower and bulwarks.

Verse 3

3 Moreover take thou unto thee an iron pan, and set it for a wall of iron between thee and the city: and set thy face against it, and it shall be besieged, and thou shalt lay siege against it. This shall be a sign to the house of Israel.

A wall — That it may resemble a wall of iron, for as impregnable as such a wall, shall the resolution and patience of the Chaldeans be.

Verse 4

4 Lie thou also upon thy left side, and lay the iniquity of the house of Israel upon it: according to the number of the days that thou shalt lie upon it thou shalt bear their iniquity.

Lay — Take upon thee the representation of their guilt and punishment.

House of Israel — The ten tribes.

The number — By this thou shalt intimate how long I have borne with their sins, and how long they shall bear their punishment.

Verse 5

5 For I have laid upon thee the years of their iniquity, according to the number of the days, three hundred and ninety days: so shalt thou bear the iniquity of the house of Israel.

I have laid — I have pointed out the number of years wherein apostate Israel sinned against me, and I did bear with them.

Years — These years probably began at Solomon's falling to idolatry, in the twenty-seventh year of his reign, and ended in the fifth of Zedekiah's captivity.

Verse 6

6 And when thou hast accomplished them, lie again on thy right side, and thou shalt bear the iniquity of the house of Judah forty days: I have appointed thee each day for a year.

Accomplished — That is, almost accomplished.

House of Judah — Of the two tribes.

Forty days — Probably from Josiah's renewing the covenant, until the destruction of the temple, during which time God deferred to punish, expecting whether they would keep their covenant, or retain their idolatries, which latter they did for thirteen years of Josiah's reign, for eleven of Jehoiakim's, and eleven of Zedekiah's reign, and five of his captivity, which amount to just forty years. But all this was done in a vision.

Verse 7

7 Therefore thou shalt set thy face toward the siege of Jerusalem, and thine arm shall be uncovered, and thou shalt prophesy against it.

Set — While thou liest on thy side thou shalt fix thy countenance on the portrait of besieged Jerusalem.

Uncovered — Naked and stretched out as being ready to strike.

Verse 8

8 And, behold, I will lay bands upon thee, and thou shalt not turn thee from one side to another, till thou hast ended the days of thy siege.

Bands — An invisible restraint assuring him, that those could no more remove from the siege, than he from that side he lay on.

Verse 9

9 Take thou also unto thee wheat, and barley, and beans, and lentiles, and millet, and fitches, and put them in one vessel, and make thee bread thereof, according to the number of the days that thou shalt lie upon thy side, three hundred and ninety days shalt thou eat thereof.

Take — Provide thee corn enough: for a grievous famine will accompany the siege.

Wheat — All sorts of grain are to be provided, and all will be little enough.

One vessel — Mix the worst with the best to lengthen out the provision.

Verse 10

10 And thy meat which thou shalt eat shall be by weight, twenty shekels a day: from time to time shalt thou eat it.

By weight — Not as much as you will, but a small pittance delivered by weight to all.

Twenty shekels — Ten ounces: scarce enough to maintain life.

From time to time — At set hours this was weighed out.

Verse 11

11 Thou shalt drink also water by measure, the sixth part of an hin: from time to time shalt thou drink.

The sixth part — About six ounces.

Verse 12

12 And thou shalt eat it as barley cakes, and thou shalt bake it with dung that cometh out of man, in their sight.

As barley cakes — Because they never had enough to make a loaf with, they eat them as barley cakes.

With dung — There was no wood left, nor yet dung of other creatures. This also was represented in a vision.

Verse 17

17 That they may want bread and water, and be astonied one with another, and consume away for their iniquity.

May want — So because they served not God with chearfulness in the abundance of all things, He made them serve their enemies in the want of all things.

Chapter Five

The destruction of Jerusalem, represented by a sign, the cutting and burning and scattering of hair, ver. 1 - 4.
Sin, the cause of this destruction, ver. 5 - 7.
Wrath, misery and ruin threatened, ver. 8 - 15.

Verse 1

1 And thou, son of man, take thee a sharp knife, take thee a barber's razor, and cause it to pass upon thine head and upon thy beard: then take thee balances to weigh, and divide the hair.

Take — Thus foretel the mourning, reproach, and deformity that are coming, for all this is signified by shaving the head and beard.

Verse 2

2 Thou shalt burn with fire a third part in the midst of the city, when the days of the siege are fulfilled: and thou shalt take a third part, and smite about it with a knife: and a third part thou shalt scatter in the wind; and I will draw out a sword after them.

A third part — Described on the tile, chap. 4:1, a type of what should be done in Jerusalem.

The days — When the three hundred and ninety days of thy lying against the portrayed city shall be ended.

With a knife — To signify them that fall by the sword.

Scatter — To typify them that fell to the Chaldeans, or fled to Egypt, or other countries.

Verse 3

3 Thou shalt also take thereof a few in number, and bind them in thy skirts.

Take — Of the last third.

Bind — As men tied up in the skirt of their garment what they would not lose: to signify the small remnant.

Verse 4

4 Then take of them again, and cast them into the midst of the fire, and burn them in the fire; for thereof shall a fire come forth into all the house of Israel.

Of them — Out of that little remnant.

In the fire — For their sin against God, their discontents at their state, and conspiracies against their governor, another fire shall break out which shall devour the most, and be near consuming all the houses of Israel.

Verse 5

5 Thus saith the Lord GOD; This is Jerusalem: I have set it in the midst of the nations and countries that are round about her.

This is Jerusalem — This portrayed city, is typically Jerusalem.

The midst — Jerusalem was set in the midst of the nations, to be as the heart in the body, to invigorate the dead world with a divine life, as well as to enlighten the dark world with a divine light.

Verse 6

6 And she hath changed my judgments into wickedness more than the nations, and my statutes more than the countries that are round about her: for they have refused my judgments and my statutes, they have not walked in them.

More — More than the heathen.

Verse 7

7 Therefore thus saith the Lord GOD; Because ye multiplied more than the nations that are round about you, and have not walked in my statutes, neither have kept my judgments, neither have done according to the judgments of the nations that are round about you;

Multiplied — In idols, superstitions, and wickedness.

Neither — You have exceeded them in superstition and idolatry, and fallen short of them in moral virtues.

Verse 9

9 And I will do in thee that which I have not done, and whereunto I will not do any more the like, because of all thine abominations.

Not done — Though the old world perished by water, and Sodom by fire, yet neither one or other was so lingering a death.

Verse 10

10 Therefore the fathers shall eat the sons in the midst of thee, and the sons shall eat their fathers; and I will execute judgments in thee, and the whole remnant of thee will I scatter into all the winds.

Scatter — This was verified when they were fetched away, who were left at the departure of the besiegers, and when the very small remnant with Johanan fled into Egypt.

Verse 11

11 Wherefore, as I live, saith the Lord GOD; Surely, because thou hast defiled my sanctuary with all thy detestable things, and with all thine abominations, therefore will I also diminish thee; neither shall mine eye spare, neither will I have any pity.

Sanctuary — My temple.

Detestable things — Thy idols.

Verse 13

13 Thus shall mine anger be accomplished, and I will cause my fury to rest upon them, and I will be comforted: and they shall know that I the LORD have spoken it in my zeal, when I have accomplished my fury in them.

Comforted — In executing my vengeance.

In my zeal — For my own glory.

Verse 15

15 So it shall be a reproach and a taunt, an instruction and an astonishment unto the nations that are round about thee, when I shall execute judgments in thee in anger and in fury and in furious rebukes. I the LORD have spoken it.

Taunt — A very proverb among them.

Instruction — Sinners shall learn by thy miseries, what they may expect from me.

Verse 17

17 So will I send upon you famine and evil beasts, and they shall bereave thee; and pestilence and blood shall pass through thee; and I will bring the sword upon thee. I the LORD have spoken it.

Bereave thee — Of your children, friends, and your own life.

Pestilence and blood — Thy land shall be the common road for pestilence and blood. Tho' this prophecy was to be accomplished presently, in the destruction of Jerusalem by the Chaldeans; yet it may well be supposed to look forward, to the final destruction of it by the Romans, when God made a full end of the Jewish nation, and caused his fury to rest upon them.

Chapter Six

A threatening of the destruction of Israel for their idolatry, ver. 1 - 7.
A promise of the gracious return of a remnant, ver. 8 - 10.
Directions to lament the sins and calamities of Israel, ver. 11 - 14.

Verse 2

2 Son of man, set thy face toward the mountains of Israel, and prophesy against them,

The mountains — The inhabitants of the mountains, who were secure in their fastnesses.

Verse 3

3 And say, Ye mountains of Israel, hear the word of the Lord GOD; Thus saith the Lord GOD to the mountains, and to the hills, to the rivers, and to the valleys; Behold, I, even I, will bring a sword upon you, and I will destroy your high places.

Rivers — To those who dwell by river sides, or in the valleys.

High places — The places of your idolatrous worship.

Verse 4

4 And your altars shall be desolate, and your images shall be broken: and I will cast down your slain men before your idols.

Cast down — Before the altars of your idols, which you fly to for refuge.

Verse 5

5 And I will lay the dead carcases of the children of Israel before their idols; and I will scatter your bones round about your altars.

And — Thus the idols were upbraided with their inability to help their worshippers, and the idolaters, with the folly of trusting in them.

Verse 6

6 In all your dwellingplaces the cities shall be laid waste, and the high places shall be desolate; that your altars may be laid waste and made desolate, and your idols may be broken and cease, and your images may be cut down, and your works may be abolished.

Your works — All your costly work for your idols.

Verse 8

8 Yet will I leave a remnant, that ye may have some that shall escape the sword among the nations, when ye shall be scattered through the countries.

Remnant — It is the Lord that preserves a remnant, the enemies rage would destroy all.

Verse 9

9 And they that escape of you shall remember me among the nations whither they shall be carried captives, because I am broken with their whorish heart, which hath departed from me, and with their eyes, which go a whoring after their idols: and they shall lothe themselves for the evils which they have committed in all their abominations.

Shall remember — So as to turn unto me.

Broken — I am much grieved.

Whorish heart — Idolatrous hearts depart from God, as an adulterous wife departs from her husband.

Loath — With a mixture of grief towards God, of indignation against themselves, and abhorrence of the offence.

Verse 10

10 And they shall know that I am the LORD, and that I have not said in vain that I would do this evil unto them.

In vain — Either without cause, the sufferers gave him just cause to pronounce that evil; or without effect. Their sins where the cause, and their destruction is the effect of their sufferings.

Verse 11

11 Thus saith the Lord GOD; Smite with thine hand, and stamp with thy foot, and say, Alas for all the evil abominations of the house of Israel! for they shall fall by the sword, by the famine, and by the pestilence.

Smite — To shew thy wonder, indignation, sorrow, and pity, for their sins and sufferings.

Verse 12

12 He that is far off shall die of the pestilence; and he that is near shall fall by the sword; and he that remaineth and is besieged shall die by the famine: thus will I accomplish my fury upon them.

Far off — Either by flight, or captivity.

Shall fall — Who dwell near to Jerusalem, or would retire to it, when the Babylonians approach.

Verse 14

14 So will I stretch out my hand upon them, and make the land desolate, yea, more desolate than the wilderness toward Diblath, in all their habitations: and they shall know that I am the LORD.

Wilderness — The horrid wilderness of Moab. Therein the fiery serpents so much annoyed Israel. Accordingly the land of Canaan is at this day one of the most desolate countries in the world.

Chapter Seven

In this chapter the prophet tells them, that a final ruin is coming, ver. 1 - 6.
A ruin just at the door, ver. 7 - 10.
An unavoidable ruin, because of their sins, ver. 11 - 15.
That their strength and wealth would be no fence against it, ver. 16 - 19. That the temple, which they trusted in, should itself be ruined, ver. 20 - 22. That it should be an universal ruin, the sin that brought it being universal, ver, 23 - 27.

Verse 1

1 Moreover the word of the LORD came unto me, saying,

An end — An end of God's patience, and of the peace and welfare of the people.

Verse 4

4 And mine eye shall not spare thee, neither will I have pity: but I will recompense thy ways upon thee, and thine abominations shall be in the midst of thee: and ye shall know that I am the LORD.

Recompense — The punishment of them.

Verse 5

5 Thus saith the Lord GOD; An evil, an only evil, behold, is come.

An evil — An evil and sore affliction, a singular, uncommon one.

Verse 6

6 An end is come, the end is come: it watcheth for thee; behold, it is come.

An end — When the end is come upon the wicked world, then an only evil comes upon it. The sorest of temporal judgments have their allays; but the torments of the damned are an evil, an only evil.

Verse 7

7 The morning is come unto thee, O thou that dwellest in the land: the time is come, the day of trouble is near, and not the sounding again of the mountains.

The morning — The fatal morning, the day of destruction.

Sounding — Not a mere echo, not a fancy, but a real thing.

Verse 10

10 Behold the day, behold, it is come: the morning is gone forth; the rod hath blossomed, pride hath budded.

Is come — Of your wickedness; pride and violence in particular.

Verse 11

11 Violence is risen up into a rod of wickedness: none of them shall remain, nor of their multitude, nor of any of theirs: neither shall there be wailing for them.

None — They shall be utterly wasted for their sins.

Wailing — The living shall not bewail their dead friends, because they shall judge the dead in a better case than the living.

Verse 12

12 The time is come, the day draweth near: let not the buyer rejoice, nor the seller mourn: for wrath is upon all the multitude thereof.

Mourn — Men usually part with their estates grieving that they must transmit their right to others; but let them now think how little a while they could have kept them, and how little time they shall keep them who have bought them.

Verse 13

13 For the seller shall not return to that which is sold, although they were yet alive: for the vision is touching the whole multitude thereof, which shall not return; neither shall any strengthen himself in the iniquity of his life.

Yet alive — For if any should survive the captivity, yet the conqueror wasting and destroying all, would confound all ancient boundaries.

Touching — The evils threatened are designed against all the multitude of Israel.

Strengthen — Nor shall any one man of them all be able to secure himself, by any sinful contrivance.

Verse 14

14 They have blown the trumpet, even to make all ready; but none goeth to the battle: for my wrath is upon all the multitude thereof.

They — The house of Israel have summoned in all fit for arms.

None — There is not a man going to the war.

Wrath — That displeasure which takes away their courage.

Verse 15

15 The sword is without, and the pestilence and the famine within: he that is in the field shall die with the sword; and he that is in the city, famine and pestilence shall devour him.

Without — In the countries.

Within — The besieged city.

Field — Whoever is in the field.

Verse 16

16 But they that escape of them shall escape, and shall be on the mountains like doves of the valleys, all of them mourning, every one for his iniquity.

Iniquity — Either for the punishment of their iniquity, or for their iniquity itself.

Verse 18

18 They shall also gird themselves with sackcloth, and horror shall cover them; and shame shall be upon all faces, and baldness upon all their heads.

Baldness — Either by pulling off the hair amidst their sorrows, or cutting it off in token of mourning.

Verse 19

19 They shall cast their silver in the streets, and their gold shall be removed: their silver and their gold shall not be able to deliver them in the day of the wrath of the LORD: they shall not satisfy their souls, neither fill their bowels: because it is the stumblingblock of their iniquity.

Cast — That they may be the lighter to fly.

Removed — Carried away into Babylon.

Not satisfy — They shall afford them no comfort.

Stumbling-block — This silver and gold they coveted immeasurably, and abused to pride, luxury, idolatry and oppression; this that they stumbled at and fell into sin, now they stumble at and fall into the deepest misery.

Verse 20

20 As for the beauty of his ornament, he set it in majesty: but they made the images of their abominations and of their detestable things therein: therefore have I set it far from them.

The beauty — The temple, and all that pertained to it, which was the beauty and glory of that nation.

He set — God commanded it should be beautiful and magnificent.

Images — Their idols.

Far from them — I have sent them far from the temple.

Verse 21

21 And I will give it into the hands of the strangers for a prey, and to the wicked of the earth for a spoil; and they shall pollute it.

It — My temple.

Verse 22

22 My face will I turn also from them, and they shall pollute my secret place: for the robbers shall enter into it, and defile it.

Turn — Either from the Jews, or from the Chaldeans, neither relieving the one nor restraining the other.

Secret place — The temple, and the holy of holies.

Robbers — The soldiers.

Verse 23

23 Make a chain: for the land is full of bloody crimes, and the city is full of violence.

A chain — To bind the captives.

Verse 24

24 Wherefore I will bring the worst of the heathen, and they shall possess their houses: I will also make the pomp of the strong to cease; and their holy places shall be defiled.

The pomp — The magnificence and glory, wherein they boasted; or the temple that the Jews gloried in.

Verse 26

26 Mischief shall come upon mischief, and rumour shall be upon rumour; then shall they seek a vision of the prophet; but the law shall perish from the priest, and counsel from the ancients.

Seek — But in vain.

The priest — He shall have no words either of counsel or comfort to say to them.

Ancients — Nor shall their senators know what to advise.

Verse 27

27 The king shall mourn, and the prince shall be clothed with desolation, and the hands of the people of the land shall be troubled: I will do unto them after their way, and according to their deserts will I judge them; and they shall know that I am the LORD.

The king — Zedekiah.

The prince — Every magistrate.

Troubled — Hang down, and melt away. What can men contrive or do for themselves, when God is departed from them? All must needs be in tears, all in trouble, when God comes to judge them according to their deserts, and so make them know, that he is the Lord, to whom vengeance belongeth.

Chapter Eight

God in vision brings Ezekiel to Jerusalem, ver. 1 - 4.
There he sees the image of jealousy, ver. 5, 6.
The elders of Israel worshipping all manner of images, ver. 7 - 12.
The women weeping for Tammuz, ver. 13, 14.
The men worshiping the sun, ver. 15, 16.
Threatenings against them, ver. 17, 18.

Verse 1

1 And it came to pass in the sixth year, in the sixth month, in the fifth day of the month, as I sat in mine house, and the elders of Judah sat before me, that the hand of the Lord GOD fell there upon me.

Sixth year — Of Jeconiah's captivity.

Sixth month — Elul or our August.

The elders — The chief of those that were now in captivity. They were come either to spend the sabbath in religious exercises, or to enquire what would become of their brethren in Jerusalem.

The hand — The spirit of prophecy.

Verse 2

2 Then I beheld, and lo a likeness as the appearance of fire: from the appearance of his loins even downward, fire; and from his loins even upward, as the appearance of brightness, as the colour of amber.

A likeness — Of a man; the man whom he had seen upon the throne.

Fire — This fire might denote the wrath of God against Jerusalem.

Verse 3

3 And he put forth the form of an hand, and took me by a lock of mine head; and the spirit lifted me up between the earth and the heaven, and brought me in the visions of God to Jerusalem, to the door of the inner gate that looketh toward the north; where was the seat of the image of jealousy, which provoketh to jealousy.

And — This, and all the passages to the end of the 16th verse, was done in vision only.

Inner gate — To the door of the gate of the inner court.

The north — The temple courts had four gates towards the four quarters, and this was the north gate, which opened into the great court where Ahaz had set up his Damascen altar, and where the idols were set up.

The image — Baal, which Manasseh had set up, Josiah had destroyed, but succeeding kings had again set it up.

Jealousy — Because it was so notorious an affront to God, who had married Israel to himself.

Verse 5

5 Then said he unto me, Son of man, lift up thine eyes now the way toward the north. So I lifted up mine eyes the way toward the north, and behold northward at the gate of the altar this image of jealousy in the entry.

Northward — Ahaz had removed it from the middle of the court and set it near this north gate, to which it gave name.

Entry — In the very passage to the temple, to affront the worship of God.

Verse 6

6 He said furthermore unto me, Son of man, seest thou what they do? even the great abominations that the house of Israel committeth here, that I should go far off from my sanctuary? but turn thee yet again, and thou shalt see greater abominations.

They — The generality of the Jews.

Great abominations — The notorious idolatries.

Here — In this court, in view of my temple.

Far off — Not that they designed this, but no other could be expected.

Verse 7

7 And he brought me to the door of the court; and when I looked, behold a hole in the wall.

The door — The second door, for there were two in the north side.

Verse 8

8 Then said he unto me, Son of man, dig now in the wall: and when I had digged in the wall, behold a door.

A door — A private door, by which the priests entered into the chamber of their imagery, to perform idolatrous worship to their images.

Verse 9

9 And he said unto me, Go in, and behold the wicked abominations that they do here.

Are doing — Under the approach of judgments, in this very place, under the walls of my temple.

Verse 10

10 So I went in and saw; and behold every form of creeping things, and abominable beasts, and all the idols of the house of Israel, pourtrayed upon the wall round about.

Every form — Of such creatures as the Egyptians, or any others with whom the Jews had acquaintance, worshipped.

Verse 11

11 And there stood before them seventy men of the ancients of the house of Israel, and in the midst of them stood Jaazaniah the son of Shaphan, with every man his censer in his hand; and a thick cloud of incense went up.

Seventy — Heads of the tribes or families, who should have been examples of true religion, not ringleaders in idolatry.

Shaphan — Mentioned 2 Kings 22:9. Shaphan was forward in reforming under Josiah and his son is as forward in corrupting the worship of God.

Verse 12

12 Then said he unto me, Son of man, hast thou seen what the ancients of the house of Israel do in the dark, every man in the chambers of his imagery? for they say, The LORD seeth us not; the LORD hath forsaken the earth.

Seeth not — They deny God's care of them and their affairs, and therefore they must chuse some other god.

Verse 13

13 He said also unto me, Turn thee yet again, and thou shalt see greater abominations that they do.

Greater — Either because added to all the rest: or, because some circumstances in these make them more abominable.

Verse 14

14 Then he brought me to the door of the gate of the LORD's house which was toward the north; and, behold, there sat women weeping for Tammuz.

The door — Of the outer court, or court of the women, so called, because they were allowed to come into it.

Weeping — Performing all the lewd and beastly rites of that idol, called by the Greeks, Adonis.

Verse 15

15 Then said he unto me, Hast thou seen this, O son of man? turn thee yet again, and thou shalt see greater abominations than these.

Greater — These later wickednesses may be accounted greater, because acted in a more sacred place.

Verse 16

16 And he brought me into the inner court of the LORD's house, and, behold, at the door of the temple of the LORD, between the porch and the altar, were about five and twenty men, with their backs toward the temple of the LORD, and their faces toward the east; and they worshipped the sun toward the east.

Inner court — The innermost, that which was next the temple, called here the Lord's house.

At the door — Before he saw abominations in the gates of the courts, now he is come to the very house itself.

The porch — That stately porch, beautified with the curious and mighty brass pillars, Jachin and Boaz.

Altar — The brazen altar for burnt-offerings, which was placed in the court before the front of the temple, and is here represented in its proper place.

Their backs — In contempt of God, and his worship.

The sun — In imitation of the Persians, Egyptians, and other eastern idolaters; these Jews turn their back on God who created the sun, and worship the creature in contempt of the Creator.

Verse 17

17 Then he said unto me, Hast thou

seen this, O son of man? Is it a light thing to the house of Judah that they commit the abominations which they commit here? for they have filled the land with violence, and have returned to provoke me to anger: and, lo, they put the branch to their nose.

Violence — All injustice is here meant towards all sorts of men, whom they first despise and next destroy.

Returned — From injustice against man they return to impiety against God.

The branch — As the worshippers of Bacchus waved their Thyrsus, the stalk wreathed with ivy, and bowed their bodies and often kissed the branches, so did these idolatrous Jews.

Verse 18

18 Therefore will I also deal in fury: mine eye shall not spare, neither will I have pity: and though they cry in mine ears with a loud voice, yet will I not hear them.

Will not hear — The time was, when God was ready to have heard, even before they cried: but now they cry aloud, and yet cry in vain. It is the upright heart which God regards, and not the loud voice.

Chapter Nine

Instruments prepared to destroy the city, ver. 1 - 2.
The glory removes to the threshold of the temple, ver. 3.
Orders given to mark a remnant, ver. 3, 4.
The execution of them who were not marked begun, ver. 5 - 7.
The prophet intercedes, but in vain, ver. 8 - 10.
The report of him that had marked the remnant, ver. 11.

Verse 1

1 He cried also in mine ears with a loud voice, saying, Cause them that have charge over the city to draw near, even every man with his destroying weapon in his hand.

He — The man whom he had seen upon the throne.

Them — Those whom God hath appointed to destroy the city: perhaps angels.

Every man — Every one; 'tis an Hebrew idiom. Each of these had a weapon proper for that kind of destruction which he was to effect; and so, some to slay with the sword, another with the pestilence, another with famine.

In his hand — Denoting both expedition in, and strength for the work.

Verse 2

2 And, behold, six men came from the way of the higher gate, which lieth toward the north, and every man a slaughter weapon in his hand; and one man among them was clothed with linen, with a writer's inkhorn by his side: and they went in, and stood beside the brasen altar.

And — As soon as the command was given, the ministers of God's displeasure appear.

Men — In appearance and vision they were men, and the prophet calls them as he saw them.

The north — Insinuating whence their destruction should come.

One man — Not a companion, but as one of authority over them.

With linen — A garment proper to the priesthood.

They — All the seven.

Verse 3

3 And the glory of the God of Israel was gone up from the cherub, whereupon he was, to the threshold of the house. And he called to the man clothed with linen, which had the writer's inkhorn by his side;

The glory — The glorious brightness, such as sometimes appeared above the cherubim in the most holy place.

Gone up — Departing from the place he had so long dwelt in.

He was — Wont to sit and appear.

Threshold — Of the temple, in token of his sudden departure from the Jews, because of their sins.

Verse 4

4 And the LORD said unto him, Go through the midst of the city, through the midst of Jerusalem, and set a mark upon the foreheads of the men that sigh and that cry for all the abominations that be done in the midst thereof.

That sigh — Out of grief for other mens sins and sorrows.

Cry — Who dare openly bewail the abominations of this wicked city, and so bear their testimony against it.

Verse 5

5 And to the others he said in mine hearing, Go ye after him through the city, and smite: let not your eye spare, neither have ye pity:

The others — The six slaughter-men.

Verse 6

6 Slay utterly old and young, both maids, and little children, and women: but come not near any man upon whom is the mark; and begin at my sanctuary. Then they began at the ancient men which were before the house.

At my sanctuary — There are the great sinners, and the abominable sins which have brought this on them.

Verse 7

7 And he said unto them, Defile the house, and fill the courts with the slain: go ye forth. And they went forth, and slew in the city.

And slew — The slaughter also was in vision.

Verse 8

8 And it came to pass, while they were slaying them, and I was left, that I fell upon my face, and cried, and said, Ah Lord GOD! wilt thou destroy all the residue of Israel in thy pouring out of thy fury upon Jerusalem?

Was left — Left alone, now both the sealer, and the slayers were gone.

Chapter Ten

The scattering the coals of fire upon the city, ver. 1 - 7.
The removal of the glory of God from the temple, ver. 8 - 22.

Verse 2

2 And he spake unto the man clothed with linen, and said, Go in between the wheels, even under the cherub, and fill thine hand with coals of fire from between the cherubims, and scatter them over the city. And he went in in my sight.

He — That sat on the throne.

Scatter — That it may take fire in all parts, and none may escape.

Verse 3

3 Now the cherubims stood on the right side of the house, when the man went in; and the cloud filled the inner court.

The right side — The north-side, the side towards Babylon, from whence the fire came which consumed the city.

The man — Christ, the Lord of angels, who now attend his coming and commands.

The cloud — As the sign of God's presence.

The inner court — The court of the priests, who were chief in the apostacy.

Verse 4

4 Then the glory of the LORD went up from the cherub, and stood over the threshold of the house; and the house was filled with the cloud, and the court was full of the brightness of the LORD's glory.

The glory — The visible token of the presence of the God of glory.

Went up — In token of his departure from the temple.

And stood — Shewing his unwillingness to leave, and giving them time to return to him, he stands where he might he seen, both by priests and people, that both might be moved to repentance.

Verse 5

5 And the sound of the cherubims' wings was heard even to the outer court, as the voice of the Almighty God when he speaketh.

Was heard — As a mighty and terrible thunder.

Verse 6

6 And it came to pass, that when he had commanded the man clothed with linen, saying, Take fire from between the wheels, from between the cherubims; then he went in, and stood beside the wheels.

And stood — Either as one that deferred execution, to try whether the city would repent, or as one who was to give some farther order to the angels, that were to be the ministers of his just displeasure.

Verse 7

7 And one cherub stretched forth his hand from between the cherubims unto the fire that was between the cherubims, and took thereof, and put it into the hands of him that was clothed with linen: who took it, and went out.

One Cherub — One of the four.

And took — As a servant that reaches what his master would have.

Went out — Out of the temple.

Verse 9

9 And when I looked, behold the four wheels by the cherubims, one wheel by one cherub, and another wheel by another cherub: and the appearance of the wheels was as the colour of a beryl stone.

Looked — Attentively viewed.

Beryl stone — Of sea-green.

Verse 10

10 And as for their appearances, they four had one likeness, as if a wheel had been in the midst of a wheel.

They — The wheels. This intimates the references of providence to each other, and their dependences on each other: and the joint tendency of all to one common end, while their motions appear to us intricate and perplexed, yea, seemingly contrary.

Verse 11

11 When they went, they went upon their four sides; they turned not as they went, but to the place whither the head looked they followed it; they turned not as they went.

When — The wheels moved by the cherubim, or that spirit of life, which moved the living creatures.

They went — They were so framed, that they could move on all four sides without the difficulty and delay of turning.

Head — Of the living creatures.

Verse 12

12 And their whole body, and their backs, and their hands, and their wings, and the wheels, were full of eyes round about, even the wheels that they four had.

And — Now he describes both the cherubim and wheels as full of wisdom, and as governed by an excellent wisdom.

The wheels — Which the four cherubim had to move, govern, and direct.

Verse 13

13 As for the wheels, it was cried unto them in my hearing, O wheel.

The wheels — As to their frame and motion.

It was cried — Still there was one who guided, as by vocal direction.

Unto them — To each of them.

Verse 14

14 And every one had four faces: the first face was the face of a cherub, and the second face was the face of a man, and the third the face of a lion, and the fourth the face of an eagle.

Every one — Of the living creatures, chap. 1:6.

Verse 17

17 When they stood, these stood; and when they were lifted up, these lifted up themselves also: for the spirit of the living creature was in them.

For — There is a perfect harmony between second causes in their dependence on, and subjection to, the one infinite, wise, good, holy, and just God. The spirit of God directs all the creatures, upper and lower, so that they shall serve the divine purpose. Events are not determined by the wheel of fortune, which is blind, but by the wheels of providence, which are full of eyes.

Verse 18

18 Then the glory of the LORD departed from off the threshold of the house, and stood over the cherubims.

And stood — On the right side of the house, where the cherubim were in the inner court.

Verse 19

19 And the cherubims lifted up their wings, and mounted up from the earth in my sight: when they went out, the wheels also were beside them, and every one stood at the door of the east gate of the LORD's house; and the glory of the God of Israel was over them above.

And every one — The glory, the cherubim, the wheels, all stood, respiting execution, and giving opportunity of preventing the approaching misery.

The east gate — The last court, the court of the people.

Verse 20

20 This is the living creature that I saw under the God of Israel by the river of Chebar; and I knew that they were the cherubims.

I knew — Either by special assurance as a prophet, or by comparing them with those which he had often seen in the temple.

Chapter Eleven

God's message of wrath to those who remained secure at Jerusalem, ver. 1 - 13.
A message of comfort to the dejected captives at Babylon, ver. 14 - 21.
The glory of God removes farther, ver. 22, 23.
The vision disappears, of which Ezekiel gives an account, ver. 24, 25.

Verse 1

1 Moreover the spirit lifted me up, and brought me unto the east gate of the LORD's house, which looketh eastward: and behold at the door of the gate five and twenty men; among whom I saw Jaazaniah the son of Azur, and Pelatiah the son of Benaiah, princes of the people.

Jaazaniah — Not him that is mentioned chap. 8:11.

Pelatiah — Named here for that dreadful sudden death, whereby he became a warning to others.

Verse 2

2 Then said he unto me, Son of man, these are the men that devise mischief, and give wicked counsel in this city:

He — The Lord sitting on the cherub.

Verse 3

3 Which say, It is not near; let us build houses: this city is the caldron, and we be the flesh.

It — The threatened danger and ruin by the Chaldeans.

The caldron — This is an impious scoff, yet mixt with some fear of the prophet, Jeremiah 1:13.

Verse 6

6 Ye have multiplied your slain in this city, and ye have filled the streets thereof with the slain.

Ye — Many murders have you committed yourselves, and you are accountable to God for all those whom the Chaldeans have slain, seeing you persuaded them, thus obstinately to stand out.

Verse 7

7 Therefore thus saith the Lord GOD; Your slain whom ye have laid in the midst of it, they are the flesh, and this city is the caldron: but I will bring you forth out of the midst of it.

Bring you forth — Not in mercy, but in wrath, by the conquering hand of Babylon.

Verse 9

9 And I will bring you out of the midst thereof, and deliver you into the hands of strangers, and will execute judgments among you.

Deliver you — Defeating all your projects for escape.

Verse 10

10 Ye shall fall by the sword; I will judge you in the border of Israel; and ye shall know that I am the LORD.

Will judge — My just judgments shall pursue you, whithersoever you fly.

Verse 11

11 This city shall not be your caldron, neither shall ye be the flesh in the midst thereof; but I will judge you in the border of Israel:

Your caldron — The place of your sufferings; greater are reserved for you in a strange land.

Judge you — I will do more against you at Riblah, where the captive king had his children, and others with them, first murdered before his eyes, and then his own eyes put out; Riblah is called the border of Israel: for Syria was adjoining to Israel on the north, and Riblah was on the frontiers of Syria.

Verse 13

13 And it came to pass, when I prophesied, that Pelatiah the son of Benaiah died. Then fell I down upon my face, and cried with a loud voice, and said, Ah Lord GOD! wilt thou make a full end of the remnant of Israel?

Pelatiah — Mentioned verse 1, a principal man among the twenty-five princes, who made all the mischief in Jerusalem. It should seem this was done in vision now, (as the slaying of the ancient men, chap. 9:6,) but it was an assurance, that when this prophecy was published, it would be done in fact. And the death of Pelatiah was an earnest of the compleat accomplishment of the prophecy.

A full end — By slaying all, as this man is cut off.

Verse 15

15 Son of man, thy brethren, even thy brethren, the men of thy kindred, and all the house of Israel wholly, are they unto whom the inhabitants of Jerusalem have said, Get you far from the LORD: unto us is this land given in possession.

Thy brethren — Thy nearest kindred, which it seems were left in Jerusalem.

Their degeneracy is more noted in the repetition of the word brethren.

Gone far — Ye are gone far from the Lord; as much as the Heathens accused the Christians of atheism.

Verse 16

16 Therefore say, Thus saith the Lord GOD; Although I have cast them far off among the heathen, and although I have scattered them among the countries, yet will I be to them as a little sanctuary in the countries where they shall come.

Say — In vindication of them.

Although — The obstinate Jews at Jerusalem will call them apostates; but I the Lord sent them thither, and will own them there.

Scattered — Dispersed them in many countries which are under the king of Babylon: yet they are dear to me.

A little sanctuary — A little one in opposition to that great temple at Jerusalem. To him they shall flee, and in him they shall be safe, as he was that took hold on the horns of the altar. And they shall have such communion with God in the land of their captivity, as it was thought could be had no where but in the temple.

Verse 18

18 And they shall come thither, and they shall take away all the detestable things thereof and all the abominations thereof from thence.

They — They who assemble upon Cyrus's proclamation first, and then upon Darius's proclamation, shall overcome all difficulties, dispatch the journey, and come safely to their own land.

Take away — They shall abolish superstition and idolatry from the temple.

Verse 19

19 And I will give them one heart, and I will put a new spirit within you; and I will take the stony heart out of their flesh, and will give them an heart of flesh:

One heart — Cyrus shall give them leave, and I will give them a heart to return; and on their way shall there be great utility; and, when come to Jerusalem, they shall own me, and my laws, and with one consent, build Jerusalem and the temple, and restore true religion.

The stony — That hard, inflexible, undutiful, incorrigible disposition.

Verse 21

21 But as for them whose heart walketh after the heart of their detestable things and their abominations, I will recompense their way upon their own heads, saith the Lord GOD.

Heart — Soul and affections.

Walketh — Either secretly adhere to, or provide for the service of idols, called here detestable things.

Verse 23

23 And the glory of the LORD went up from the midst of the city, and stood upon the mountain which is on the east side of the city.

Went up — The glory of the Lord removes now out of the city, over which it had stood some time, waiting for their repentance.

The mountain — Mount Olivet. He removed thither, to be as it were within call, and ready to return, if now at length in this their day, they would have understood the things that made for their peace.

Verse 24

24 Afterwards the spirit took me up, and brought me in a vision by the Spirit of God into Chaldea, to them of the captivity. So the vision that I had seen went up from me.

The spirit — The same spirit which carried him to Jerusalem, now brings him back to Chaldea.

Went up — Was at an end.

Chapter Twelve

The prophet by removing his stuff, and quitting his lodgings is a sign of Zedekiah's flight out of Jerusalem, ver. 1 - 16.
By eating his meat with trembling, he is a sign, to set forth the famine and consternation in the city, ver. 17 - 20. An assurance that these things shall be fulfilled, ver. 21 - 28.

Verse 2

2 Son of man, thou dwellest in the midst of a rebellious house, which have eyes to see, and see not; they have ears to hear, and hear not: for they are a rebellious house.

Eyes to see — They have capacity, if they would, to understand, but they will not understand, what thou speakest.

Verse 3

3 Therefore, thou son of man, prepare thee stuff for removing, and remove by day in their sight; and thou shalt remove from thy place to another place in their sight: it may be they will consider, though they be a rebellious house.

Stuff — Vessels or instruments, wherein thou mayest put what is portable.

Verse 4

4 Then shalt thou bring forth thy stuff by day in their sight, as stuff for removing: and thou shalt go forth at even in their sight, as they that go forth into captivity.

In their sight — Before 'tis quite night, that they, who should learn by this sign, may see and consider it.

Verse 5

5 Dig thou through the wall in their sight, and carry out thereby.

Dig — Come not through the door, but as one who knows there is a guard upon the door, get to some back part of thy house, and dig there thyself, either to make the greater haste, or to keep all secret; for all will be little enough for them that must act what thou dost represent.

Carry out — Through the hole thou hast dug.

Verse 6

6 In their sight shalt thou bear it upon thy shoulders, and carry it forth in the twilight: thou shalt cover thy face, that thou see not the ground: for I have set thee for a sign unto the house of Israel.

Bare it — In testimony of the servitude they shall be reduced to, who then must do what servants or beasts were wont to be employed in.

Cover thy face — As unwilling to be seen or known.

For — I have set thee for a sign to them, and thou shalt tell them the meaning of these things in due time.

Verse 7

7 And I did so as I was commanded: I brought forth my stuff by day, as stuff for captivity, and in the even I digged through the wall with mine hand; I brought it forth in the twilight, and I bare it upon my shoulder in their sight.

I brought forth — Here is a transposing of his actions, and rehearsal of that in the first place, which was acted in the second place.

Verse 10

10 Say thou unto them, Thus saith the Lord GOD; This burden concerneth the prince in Jerusalem, and all the house of Israel that are among them.

Say — Though they enquire not, yet tell them what I mean hereby, that this prophecy is a burden which the kingdom shall groan under.

The prince — Zedekiah.

Verse 11

11 Say, I am your sign: like as I have done, so shall it be done unto them: they shall remove and go into captivity.

I am your sign — My person is the emblem of yours, and my actions of that you shall do. And the like shall be done to you, O inhabitants of Jerusalem. We cannot say concerning our dwelling place, that it is our resting place. For how far we may be tossed from it before we die, we cannot foresee.

Verse 12

12 And the prince that is among them shall bear upon his shoulder in the twilight, and shall go forth: they shall dig through the wall to carry out thereby: he shall cover his face, that he see not the ground with his eyes.

The prince — Zedekiah.

Shall bear — Disguised, as a servant, in hope to conceal himself, chuses the twilight as the time that would best favour his design.

They shall dig — This was fulfilled when they broke down the wall to fly, Jeremiah 39:4.

Cover his face — Zedekiah did by this aim at concealing himself.

Verse 13

13 My net also will I spread upon him, and he shall be taken in my snare: and I will bring him to Babylon to the land of the Chaldeans; yet shall he not see it, though he shall die there.

It — Neither the land nor the city; for his eyes will be put out at Riblah.

Verse 16

16 But I will leave a few men of them from the sword, from the famine, and from the pestilence; that they may declare all their abominations among the heathen whither they come; and they shall know that I am the LORD.

Declare — By relating those sins, for

which God was justly angry, and for which he punished them, though they were his own people.

Thy — The Chaldeans. See how God brings good out of evil! The dispersion of sinners, who had done God much dishonour and disservice in their own country, proves the dispersion of penitents, who shall do him much honour and service in other countries!

Verse 19

19 And say unto the people of the land, Thus saith the Lord GOD of the inhabitants of Jerusalem, and of the land of Israel; They shall eat their bread with carefulness, and drink their water with astonishment, that her land may be desolate from all that is therein, because of the violence of all them that dwell therein.

The people — Thy fellow captives.

And of the land — Those that dwell in the countries round about Jerusalem.

Her land — Jerusalem's land, so called because it was the head city thereof.

Desolate — Because it shortly shall be laid waste, emptied of inhabitants, wealth and plenty.

Violence — Injustice, oppression and tyranny of the Jews toward one another.

Verse 22

22 Son of man, what is that proverb that ye have in the land of Israel, saying, The days are prolonged, and every vision faileth?

That proverb — That short saying commonly used.

Days — Of wrath and vengeance, are to come a great while hence.

Every vision — Threatening vision, which Jeremiah and Ezekiel would fright us with, comes to nothing.

Verse 25

25 For I am the LORD: I will speak, and the word that I shall speak shall come to pass; it shall be no more prolonged: for in your days, O rebellious house, will I say the word, and will perform it, saith the Lord GOD.

I will speak — There has been and shall be a succession of God's ministers, by whom he will speak, to the end of the world. Even in the worst times, God left not himself without witness, but raised up men that spoke for him, and spoke from him.

Chapter Thirteen

The prophet shews the sin and punishment of the false prophets, ver. 1 - 16.
Of the false prophetesses, ver. 17 - 23.

Verse 2

2 Son of man, prophesy against the prophets of Israel that prophesy, and say thou unto them that prophesy out of their own hearts, Hear ye the word of the LORD;

That prophesy — Out of their own deceiving hearts, not from God.

Verse 3

3 Thus saith the Lord GOD; Woe unto the foolish prophets, that follow their own spirit, and have seen nothing!

Foolish prophets — Foolish prophets

are not of God's sending: for whom he sends, he either finds fit, or makes fit. Where he gives warrant, he gives wisdom.

Their own spirit — Not the spirit of God.

Seen nothing — God hath shewed them no vision.

Verse 4

4 O Israel, thy prophets are like the foxes in the deserts.

Thy prophets — Thy prophets, not mine.

Like the foxes — Hungry, and ravening, crafty, and guileful.

In the deserts — Where want makes them more eager after their prey.

Verse 5

5 Ye have not gone up into the gaps, neither made up the hedge for the house of Israel to stand in the battle in the day of the LORD.

Ye — Vain prophets.

Gone up — As in a besieged city, whose wall is broken down, a valiant soldier would run up into the breach to repel the enemy; so true prophets partly by prayer, and partly by doctrine, labour to preserve God's people.

Hedge — The house of Israel is the Lord's vineyard, through the hedge whereof many breaches are made.

To stand — Not with arms, but with fasting, prayer, and repentance.

Verse 6

6 They have seen vanity and lying divination, saying, The LORD saith: and the LORD hath not sent them: and they have made others to hope that they would confirm the word.

Vanity — Things that have no foundation.

Verse 9

9 And mine hand shall be upon the prophets that see vanity, and that divine lies: they shall not be in the assembly of my people, neither shall they be written in the writing of the house of Israel, neither shall they enter into the land of Israel; and ye shall know that I am the Lord GOD.

Mine hand — My power striking them.

In the assembly — Have no seat among the rulers, nor voice among the counsellors.

Written — Not registered among those that return, Ezra 2:1,2.

Enter — They shall never come into the land of Israel. They shall not be written in the book of eternal life, which is written for the just ones of the house of Israel, saith the Chaldea paraphrast.

Verse 10

10 Because, even because they have seduced my people, saying, Peace; and there was no peace; and one built up a wall, and, lo, others daubed it with untempered morter:

Peace — They told sinners, no harm would happen to them. And those are the most dangerous seducers, who suggest to sinners that which tends to lessen their dread of sin, or their fear of God. These are compared to men who build a slight tottering wall, which others daub with untempered mortar; sorry stuff, that will not bind, nor hold the bricks together: doctrines not grounded on the word of God.

Verse 14

14 So will I break down the wall that ye have daubed with untempered morter, and bring it down to the ground, so that the foundation thereof shall be discovered, and it shall fall, and ye shall be consumed in the midst thereof: and ye shall know that I am the LORD.

Ye shall know — Those that deceived others, will in the end be found to have deceived themselves. And no doom will be more fearful, than that of unfaithful ministers.

Verse 15

15 Thus will I accomplish my wrath upon the wall, and upon them that have daubed it with untempered morter, and will say unto you, The wall is no more, neither they that daubed it;

Accomplish — Fulfil what my prophets foretold.

Verse 18

18 And say, Thus saith the Lord GOD; Woe to the women that sew pillows to all armholes, and make kerchiefs upon the head of every stature to hunt souls! Will ye hunt the souls of my people, and will ye save the souls alive that come unto you?

Sew pillows — A figurative speech, expressing the security, which they promised to every one that came to them.

Kerchiefs — Triumphal caps, which were made by these prophetesses, and put upon the head of every who one consulted them, and by these they were to interpret, as a promise of victory over the Babylonians.

Stature — That is, of every age, whether younger or elder, which usually is seen by their stature.

To hunt — All this is really spreading a net, as hunters do, to catch the prey.

Will ye save — Can you preserve them alive, whom you deceive by your promises?

Verse 19

19 And will ye pollute me among my people for handfuls of barley and for pieces of bread, to slay the souls that should not die, and to save the souls alive that should not live, by your lying to my people that hear your lies?

Pollute me — Pretending my name for what I never spake.

My people — My own people.

Handfuls of barley — For a mean reward.

To slay — You denounce evil to the best, whom God wilt keep alive.

To save — Declaring safety, to the worst, whom God will destroy.

Verse 20

20 Wherefore thus saith the Lord GOD; Behold, I am against your pillows, wherewith ye there hunt the souls to make them fly, and I will tear them from your arms, and will let the souls go, even the souls that ye hunt to make them fly.

39

There — At Jerusalem.

Grow — You promise a flourishing, growing, state to all enquirers; and this is the net with which you hunt souls.

Tear them — With violence, and suddenness.

Verse 23

23 Therefore ye shall see no more vanity, nor divine divinations: for I will deliver my people out of your hand: and ye shall know that I am the LORD.

See no more vanityl-They shall see all their predictions vanish, which shall so confound them, that they shall pretend no more to visions.

Chapter Fourteen

The elders of Israel come to enquire of the prophet, ver. 1 - 5.
They are ordered to repent, or not to pretend to enquire of God, ver. 6 - 11.
Tho' Noah, Daniel and Job were to pray for the people, yet they would not prevail, ver. 12 - 21.
Yet a remnant shall escape, ver. 22, 23.

Verse 1

1 Then came certain of the elders of Israel unto me, and sat before me.

Elders — Men of note, that were in office and power among the Jews, who were come from Jerusalem.

Verse 3

3 Son of man, these men have set up their idols in their heart, and put the stumblingblock of their iniquity before their face: should I be enquired of at all by them?

Set up — Are resolved idolaters.

The stumbling block — Their idols which were both the object of their sin, and occasion of their ruin.

Verse 4

4 Therefore speak unto them, and say unto them, Thus saith the Lord GOD; Every man of the house of Israel that setteth up his idols in his heart, and putteth the stumblingblock of his iniquity before his face, and cometh to the prophet; I the LORD will answer him that cometh according to the multitude of his idols;

According — According to his desert, I will give answer, but in just judgment.

Verse 5

5 That I may take the house of Israel in their own heart, because they are all estranged from me through their idols.

Take — That I may lay open what is in their heart, and discover their hypocrisy, and impiety.

Through their idols — It is always through some idol or other, that the hearts of men are estranged from God: some creature has gained that place in the heart, which belongs to none but God.

Verse 7

7 For every one of the house of Israel, or of the stranger that sojourneth in Israel, which separateth himself from me, and setteth up his idols in his heart, and putteth the stumblingblock of his iniquity before his face, and cometh to a prophet to enquire of him concerning me; I the LORD will answer him by myself:

The stranger — Every proselyte.

I the Lord — He shall find by the answer, 'twas not the prophet, but God that answered: so dreadful, searching, and astonishing shall my answer be.

Verse 8

8 And I will set my face against that man, and will make him a sign and a proverb, and I will cut him off from the midst of my people; and ye shall know that I am the LORD.

A sign — Of divine vengeance.

Verse 9

9 And if the prophet be deceived when he hath spoken a thing, I the LORD have deceived that prophet, and I will stretch out my hand upon him, and will destroy him from the midst of my people Israel.

The prophet — The false prophet, who speaks all serene, and quiet, in hope of reward.

Have deceived — Permitted him to err, or justly left him in his blindness.

Verse 13

13 Son of man, when the land sinneth against me by trespassing grievously, then will I stretch out mine hand upon it, and will break the staff of the bread thereof, and will send famine upon it, and will cut off man and beast from it:

When — At what time soever.

Verse 14

14 Though these three men, Noah, Daniel, and Job, were in it, they should deliver but their own souls by their righteousness, saith the Lord GOD.

Noah — Who 'tis probable prevailed with God to spare the world for some years, and saved his near relations when the flood came.

Daniel — Who prevailed for the life of the wise men of Chaldea.

Job — Who daily offered sacrifice for his children, and at last reconciled God to those that had offended.

Verse 17

17 Or if I bring a sword upon that land, and say, Sword, go through the land; so that I cut off man and beast from it:

That land — What land soever it be.

Verse 19

19 Or if I send a pestilence into that land, and pour out my fury upon it in blood, to cut off from it man and beast:

In blood — In death and destruction, not by the sword.

Verse 21

21 For thus saith the Lord GOD; How much more when I send my four sore judgments upon Jerusalem, the sword, and the famine, and the noisome beast, and the pestilence, to cut off from it man and beast?

How much more — If they could not be able to keep off one of the four, how much less would they be able to keep off all four, when I commission them all to go at once.

Verse 22

22 Yet, behold, therein shall be left a remnant that shall be brought forth, both sons and daughters: behold, they shall come forth unto you, and ye shall see their way and their doings: and ye shall be comforted concerning the evil that I have brought upon Jerusalem, even concerning all that I have brought upon it.

Their way — Their sin and their punishment.

Comforted — In this proof of the truth of God.

Verse 23

23 And they shall comfort you, when ye see their ways and their doings: and ye shall know that I have not done without cause all that I have done in it, saith the Lord GOD.

Comfort you — That is, you will be comforted, when you compare their case with your own: when they tell you how righteous God was, in bringing these judgments upon them. This will reconcile you to the justice of God, in thus punishing his own people, and to the goodness of God, who now appeared to have had kind intentions in all.

Chapter Fifteen

God by the similitude of a vine, foreshews the utter destruction of Jerusalem, ver. 1 - 8.

Verse 2

2 Son of man, What is the vine tree more than any tree, or than a branch which is among the trees of the forest?

The vine-tree — Israel is here compared to a vine, which, when fruitless, is utterly unprofitable. This the prophet minds them of to humble them, and awaken them to fruitfulness.

A branch — One branch of a tree in the forest is of more use than the whole vine-tree is, except for its fruit.

Verse 3

3 Shall wood be taken thereof to do any work? or will men take a pin of it to hang any vessel thereon?

A pin — Will it afford even a pin to drive into a wall or post, on which you may safely fasten any weight.

Verse 4

4 Behold, it is cast into the fire for fuel; the fire devoureth both the ends of it, and the midst of it is burned. Is it meet for any work?

For fuel — When for its barrenness it is cut down, it is fit only to burn.

Verse 6

6 Therefore thus saith the Lord GOD; As the vine tree among the trees of the forest, which I have given to the fire for fuel, so will I give the inhabitants of Jerusalem.

Given — Doomed for food to the fire.

Verse 8

8 And I will make the land desolate, because they have committed a trespass, saith the Lord GOD.

Because — They have been so perpetually trespassing, that it seems a continued act.

Chapter Sixteen

The mean beginning of the Jewish church and nation, ver. 1 - 5.
The many favours God bestowed upon them, ver. 6 - 14.
Their treacherous and ungrateful

requital, ver. 15 - 34.

Terrible judgments threatened, ver. 35 - 43.

An aggravation of their sin and of their punishment, ver. 44 - 59.

A promise of mercy to a remnant, ver. 60 - 63.

Verse 3

3 And say, Thus saith the Lord GOD unto Jerusalem; Thy birth and thy nativity is of the land of Canaan; thy father was an Amorite, and thy mother an Hittite.

Jerusalem — The whole race of the Jews.

Thy birth — Thy root whence thou didst spring.

Thy father — Abraham, before God called him, (as his father and kindred) worshipped strange gods beyond the river, Joshua 24:14.

An Amorite — This comprehended all the rest of the cursed nations.

Verse 4

4 And as for thy nativity, in the day thou wast born thy navel was not cut, neither wast thou washed in water to supple thee; thou wast not salted at all, nor swaddled at all.

In the day — In the day I called Abraham to leave his idolatry.

Salted — Salt was used to purge, dry, and strengthen the new-born child.

Nor swaddled — So forlorn was the state of the Jews in their birth, without beauty, without strength, without friend.

Verse 5

5 None eye pitied thee, to do any of these unto thee, to have compassion upon thee; but thou wast cast out in the open field, to the lothing of thy person, in the day that thou wast born.

To the loathing — In contempt of thee as unlovely and worthless; and in abhorrence of thee as loathsome to the beholder. This seems to have reference to the exposing of the male children of the Israelites in Egypt. And it is an apt illustration of the Natural State of all the children of men. In the day that we were born, we were shapen in iniquity: our understandings darkened, our minds alienated from the life of God: all polluted with sin, which rendered us loathsome in the eyes of God.

Verse 6

6 And when I passed by thee, and saw thee polluted in thine own blood, I said unto thee when thou wast in thy blood, Live; yea, I said unto thee when thou wast in thy blood, Live.

When I passed by — God here speaks after the manner of men.

Live — This is such a command as sends forth a power to effect what is commanded; he gave that life: he spake, and it was done.

Verse 7

7 I have caused thee to multiply as the bud of the field, and thou hast increased and waxen great, and thou art come to excellent ornaments: thy breasts are fashioned, and thine hair is grown, whereas thou wast naked and bare.

Thou art come — Thou wast adorned with the choicest blessings of Divine

Providence.

Thy breasts — Grown up and fashioned under God's own hand in order to be solemnly affianced to God.

Verse 8

8 Now when I passed by thee, and looked upon thee, behold, thy time was the time of love; and I spread my skirt over thee, and covered thy nakedness: yea, I sware unto thee, and entered into a covenant with thee, saith the Lord GOD, and thou becamest mine.

When I passed — This second passing by, may be understood of God's visiting and calling them out of Egypt.

Thy time — The time of thy misery was the time of love in me towards thee.

I spread my skirt — Espoused thee, as Ruth 3:9.

Entered into a covenant — This was done at mount Sinai, when the covenant between God and Israel was sealed and ratified. Those to whom God gives spiritual life, he takes into covenant with himself. By this covenant they become his, his subjects and servants; that speaks their duty: and at the same time his portion, his treasure; that speaks their privilege.

Verse 9

9 Then washed I thee with water; yea, I throughly washed away thy blood from thee, and I anointed thee with oil.

Washed — It was a very ancient custom among the eastern people, to purify virgins who were to be espoused.

And I anointed — They were anointed that were to be married, as Ruth 3:3.

Verse 10

10 I clothed thee also with broidered work, and shod thee with badgers' skin, and I girded thee about with fine linen, and I covered thee with silk.

Broidered — Rich and beautiful needle-work.

Badgers skin — The eastern people had an art of curiously dressing and colouring the skins of those beasts, of which they made their neatest shoes, for the richest and greatest personages.

Verse 11

11 I decked thee also with ornaments, and I put bracelets upon thy hands, and a chain on thy neck.

A chain — Of gold, in token of honour and authority.

Verse 14

14 And thy renown went forth among the heathen for thy beauty: for it was perfect through my comeliness, which I had put upon thee, saith the Lord GOD.

My comeliness — "That is, thro' the beauty of their holiness, as they were a people devoted to God. This was it that put a lustre upon all their other honours, and was indeed the perfection of their beauty. Sanctified souls are truly beautiful in God's sight, and they themselves may take the comfort of it. But God must have all the glory for whatever comeliness they have, it is that which God has put upon them."

Verse 15

15 But thou didst trust in thine own

beauty, and playedst the harlot because of thy renown, and pouredst out thy fornications on every one that passed by; his it was.

Playedst the harlot — Thou didst go a whoring after idols.

Thy renown — Her renown abroad drew to her idolatrous strangers, who brought their idols with them.

Pouredst out — Didst readily prostitute thyself to them; every stranger, who passed thro' thee, might find room for his idol, and idolatry.

He it was — Thy person was at the command of every adulterer.

Verse 16

16 And of thy garments thou didst take, and deckedst thy high places with divers colours, and playedst the harlot thereupon: the like things shall not come, neither shall it be so.

Thy garments — Those costly, royal robes, the very wedding clothes.

High places — Where the idol was.

With divers colours — With those beautiful clothes I put upon thee.

The like things — As there was none before her that had done thus, so shall there be none to follow her in these things.

Verse 17

17 Thou hast also taken thy fair jewels of my gold and of my silver, which I had given thee, and madest to thyself images of men, and didst commit whoredom with them,

Images — Statues, molten and graven images.

Commit whoredom — Idolatry, spiritual adultery. And possibly here is an allusion to the rites of Adonis, or the images of Priapus.

Verse 18

18 And tookest thy broidered garments, and coveredst them: and thou hast set mine oil and mine incense before them.

Coveredst — Didst clothe the images thou hadst made.

Set mine oil — In lamps to burn before them.

Verse 19

19 My meat also which I gave thee, fine flour, and oil, and honey, wherewith I fed thee, thou hast even set it before them for a sweet savour: and thus it was, saith the Lord GOD.

For a sweet savour — To gain the favour of the idol.

Thus it was — All which is undeniable.

Verse 20

20 Moreover thou hast taken thy sons and thy daughters, whom thou hast borne unto me, and these hast thou sacrificed unto them to be devoured. Is this of thy whoredoms a small matter,

And those — These very children of mine hast thou destroyed.

Sacrificed — Not only consecrating them to be priests to dumb idols; but even burning them in sacrifice to Molech.

Devoured — Consumed to ashes.

Is this — Were thy whoredoms a small matter, that thou hast proceeded to this unnatural cruelty?

Verse 21

21 That thou hast slain my children, and delivered them to cause them to pass through the fire for them?

For them — For the idols.

Verse 24

24 That thou hast also built unto thee an eminent place, and hast made thee an high place in every street.

In every street — Idol temples were in every street; both in Jerusalem and her cities.

Verse 25

25 Thou hast built thy high place at every head of the way, and hast made thy beauty to be abhorred, and hast opened thy feet to every one that passed by, and multiplied thy whoredoms.

At every head of the way — Not content with what was done in the city, she built her idol temples in the country, wherever it was likely passengers would come.

Verse 26

26 Thou hast also committed fornication with the Egyptians thy neighbours, great of flesh; and hast increased thy whoredoms, to provoke me to anger.

Great of flesh — Naturally of a big, make, and men of great stature.

Verse 30

30 How weak is thine heart, saith the Lord GOD, seeing thou doest all these things, the work of an imperious whorish woman;

How weak — Unstable, like water.

An imperious woman — A woman, that knows no superior, nor will be neither guided nor governed.

Verse 31

31 In that thou buildest thine eminent place in the head of every way, and makest thine high place in every street; and hast not been as an harlot, in that thou scornest hire;

Not as an harlot — Common harlots make gain of their looseness, and live by that gain; thou dost worse, thou lavishest out thy credit, wealth, and all, to maintain thine adulterers.

Verse 34

34 And the contrary is in thee from other women in thy whoredoms, whereas none followeth thee to commit whoredoms: and in that thou givest a reward, and no reward is given unto thee, therefore thou art contrary.

Contrary — Here we may see, what the nature of men is, when God leaves them to themselves: yea, tho' they have the greatest advantage, to be better, and to do better.

Verse 38

38 And I will judge thee, as women that break wedlock and shed blood are judged; and I will give thee blood in fury and jealousy.

Blood — Thou gavest the blood of thy

children to idols in sacrifice; I will give thee thine own blood to drink.

Verse 42

42 So will I make my fury toward thee to rest, and my jealousy shall depart from thee, and I will be quiet, and will be no more angry.

My jealousy — The jealousy whereto you have provoked me, will never cease, 'till these judgments have utterly destroyed you, as the anger of an abused husband ceases in the publick punishment of the adulteress.

No more angry — I will no more concern myself about thee.

Verse 44

44 Behold, every one that useth proverbs shall use this proverb against thee, saying, As is the mother, so is her daughter.

The mother — Old Jerusalem, when the seat of the Jebusites, or the land of Canaan, when full of the idolatrous, bloody, barbarous nations.

Her daughter — Jerusalem, or the Jews who are more like those accursed nations in sin, than near them in place of abode.

Verse 45

45 Thou art thy mother's daughter, that lotheth her husband and her children; and thou art the sister of thy sisters, which lothed their husbands and their children: your mother was an Hittite, and your father an Amorite.

Thou — The nation of the Jews.

Thy mother's daughter — As much in thy inclinations, as for thy original.

Loatheth — That was weary of the best husband.

Verse 46

46 And thine elder sister is Samaria, she and her daughters that dwell at thy left hand: and thy younger sister, that dwelleth at thy right hand, is Sodom and her daughters.

Thine elder sister — The greater for power, riches, and numbers of people.

Her daughters — The lesser cities of the kingdom of Israel.

Thy left hand — Northward as you look toward the east.

Thy younger sister — Which was smaller and less populous.

Thy right hand — Southward from Jerusalem.

Verse 47

47 Yet hast thou not walked after their ways, nor done after their abominations: but, as if that were a very little thing, thou wast corrupted more than they in all thy ways.

Not walked after their ways — For they, all things considered, were less sinners than thou.

Nor done — Their doings were abominable, but thine have been worse.

Verse 49

49 Behold, this was the iniquity of thy sister Sodom, pride, fulness of bread, and abundance of idleness was in her and in her daughters, neither did she strengthen the hand of the poor and needy.

This was — The fountain and occasion of all.

Fulness of bread — Excess in eating and drinking.

Strengthen — She refused to help strangers.

Verse 51

51 Neither hath Samaria committed half of thy sins; but thou hast multiplied thine abominations more than they, and hast justified thy sisters in all thine abominations which thou hast done.

Hast justified — Not made them righteous, but declared them less unrighteous, than thou; of the two they are less faulty.

Verse 52

52 Thou also, which hast judged thy sisters, bear thine own shame for thy sins that thou hast committed more abominable than they: they are more righteous than thou: yea, be thou confounded also, and bear thy shame, in that thou hast justified thy sisters.

Hast judged — Condemned their apostacy, and hast judged their punishment just.

Verse 53

53 When I shall bring again their captivity, the captivity of Sodom and her daughters, and the captivity of Samaria and her daughters, then will I bring again the captivity of thy captives in the midst of them:

When — Sodom and Samaria never were restored to that state they had been in; nor were the two tribes ever made so rich, mighty, and renowned, though God brought some of them out of Babylon: the words confirm an irrecoverably low, and despised state, of the Jews in their temporals.

Then — Then, not before.

Verse 54

54 That thou mayest bear thine own shame, and mayest be confounded in all that thou hast done, in that thou art a comfort unto them.

A comfort — Encouraging sinners like those of Sodom and Samaria.

Verse 56

56 For thy sister Sodom was not mentioned by thy mouth in the day of thy pride,

Not mentioned — The sins of Sodom, and her plagues, were not minded or mentioned by thee.

Verse 57

57 Before thy wickedness was discovered, as at the time of thy reproach of the daughters of Syria, and all that are round about her, the daughters of the Philistines, which despise thee round about.

Before — The time of her pride was, when they were not yet afflicted, and despised by the Syrians.

And all — The nations that were round about and combined in league against the house of David.

Her — Syria, the chief whereof were the Philistines.

Verse 58

58 Thou hast borne thy lewdness and

thine abominations, saith the LORD.

Thy lewdness — The punishment thereof.

Verse 59

59 For thus saith the Lord GOD; I will even deal with thee as thou hast done, which hast despised the oath in breaking the covenant.

In breaking the covenant — So will I break my covenant with thee.

Verse 60

60 Nevertheless I will remember my covenant with thee in the days of thy youth, and I will establish unto thee an everlasting covenant.

Nevertheless — The Lord having denounced a perpetual punishment to the impenitent body of the Jewish nation, doth now promise to the remnant, that they shall be remembered, and obtain covenanted mercy.

My covenant — In which I promised I would not utterly cut off the seed of Israel, nor fail to send the redeemer, who should turn away iniquity from Jacob.

With thee — In the loins of Abraham, and solemnly renewed after their coming out of Egypt, which is the time, called the days of thy youth, Isaiah 44:2.

Establish — Confirm and ratify. It shall be sure, and unfailing.

An everlasting covenant — Of long continuance, as to their condition in the land of Canaan, and in what is spiritual, it shall be absolutely everlasting.

Verse 61

61 Then thou shalt remember thy ways, and be ashamed, when thou shalt receive thy sisters, thine elder and thy younger: and I will give them unto thee for daughters, but not by thy covenant.

Then — When that new covenant shall take effect.

Receive — Admit into church-communion, the Gentiles, now strangers, but then sisters.

Thine elder — Those that are greater and mightier than thou; that by their power, wealth and honour are as much above thee as the elder children are above the younger.

Thy younger — Thy lesser or meaner sister.

For daughters — As daughters hearken to, and obey, so shall the Gentiles brought into the church, hearken to the word of God, which sounded out from Jerusalem.

But not — Not by that old covenant which was violated; nor by external ceremonies, which were a great part of the first covenant, but by that covenant which writes the law in the heart, and puts the fear of God into the inward parts.

Verse 63

63 That thou mayest remember, and be confounded, and never open thy mouth any more because of thy shame, when I am pacified toward thee for all that thou hast done, saith the Lord GOD.

Open thy mouth — Neither to justify thyself, or to condemn others, or to quarrel with thy God.

Because of thy shame — Such a confusion for thy sin will cover thee. Indeed the more we feel of God's love, the more ashamed we are that ever we offended him. And the more our shame for sin is increased, the more will our comfort in God be increased also.

Chapter Seventeen

The parable of two eagles and a vine, ver. 1 - 10.
The application of it, ver. 11 - 21.
A promise to raise the house of David again, ver. 22 - 24.

Verse 2

2 Son of man, put forth a riddle, and speak a parable unto the house of Israel;

A riddle — A dark saying.

The house of Israel — The remainders of the house of Israel, whether of the ten, or of the two tribes.

Verse 3

3 And say, Thus saith the Lord GOD; A great eagle with great wings, longwinged, full of feathers, which had divers colours, came unto Lebanon, and took the highest branch of the cedar:

A great eagle — Nebuchadnezzar king of Babylon is compared to a great eagle, the king of birds, swift, strong, rapacious.

Great wings — Mighty provinces on each side of his kingdom.

Long winged — His kingdom was widely extended.

Full of feathers — And full of people.

Divers colours — Who were of divert nations, languages and manners.

Lebanon — Jerusalem the chief city of the country where this great, fruitful and pleasant hill was.

And took — Took, captive and carried away with him the king of Judah, Jehoiachin.

The cedar — The nation.

Verse 4

4 He cropped off the top of his young twigs, and carried it into a land of traffick; he set it in a city of merchants.

The top — Both the king of Judah, now eighteen years old, and the nobles and chief of the land.

Into a land — Babylon, which was a city of mighty trade.

Verse 5

5 He took also of the seed of the land, and planted it in a fruitful field; he placed it by great waters, and set it as a willow tree.

The seed — Mattaniah, whom he called Zedekiah.

Planted — Settled him on the throne of Judah.

As a willow — The prophet compares this new made king to a willow, which grows no where so well as near great waters.

Verse 6

6 And it grew, and became a spreading vine of low stature, whose branches turned toward him, and the roots thereof were under him: so it became a vine, and brought forth branches, and shot forth sprigs.

Of low stature — They grew and flourish, while they owned their state tributary to Babylon.

Toward him — Nebuchadnezzar as their protector, and sovereign lord.

The roots — All the firmness, fruitfulness, and life of this state, was in subjection to him.

Verse 7

7 There was also another great eagle with great wings and many feathers: and, behold, this vine did bend her roots toward him, and shot forth her branches toward him, that he might water it by the furrows of her plantation.

Another — The king of Egypt.

This vine — Zedekiah, his nobles and people.

Did bend — Sought his friendship.

Shot forth — Sent ambassadors, and trusted to the power of Egypt.

Water it — That they might add to their greatness, as trees grow by seasonable watering them.

By the furrows — Alluding to the manner of watering used in Egypt, by furrows or trenches to convey the water from the river Nile.

Verse 8

8 It was planted in a good soil by great waters, that it might bring forth branches, and that it might bear fruit, that it might be a goodly vine.

Was planted — By Nebuchadnezzar, in a very hopeful condition, where it might have been fruitful, and flourished.

Verse 9

9 Say thou, Thus saith the Lord GOD; Shall it prosper? shall he not pull up the roots thereof, and cut off the fruit thereof, that it wither? it shall wither in all the leaves of her spring, even without great power or many people to pluck it up by the roots thereof.

Say — Tell them what will be the issue of all this, and tell it to them in my name.

It prosper — Shall Zedekiah and his people thrive by this?

Pull up — Utterly overthrow this kingdom.

Cut Off — Put to the sword the children of Zedekiah, and of the nobles.

The leaves — All the promising hope they had shall vanish.

Without great power — The king of Babylon shall do this easily, when it is God that sends him. For God needs not great power and many people, to effect his purposes. He can without any difficulty overturn a sinful king and kingdom, and make no more of it than we do of rooting up a tree that cumbers the ground.

Verse 10

10 Yea, behold, being planted, shall it prosper? shall it not utterly wither, when the east wind toucheth it? it shall wither in the furrows where it grew.

Yea — Suppose this vine were planted

by the help of Egypt.

The east wind — When the king of Babylon, who like the blasting wind comes from the north-east, shall but touch it, it shall wither.

In the furrows — Even amidst its greatest helps, to make it flourish.

Verse 15

15 But he rebelled against him in sending his ambassadors into Egypt, that they might give him horses and much people. Shall he prosper? shall he escape that doeth such things? or shall he break the covenant, and be delivered?

He — Zedekiah.

Shall he break — Can perjury be the way for deliverance?

Verse 18

18 Seeing he despised the oath by breaking the covenant, when, lo, he had given his hand, and hath done all these things, he shall not escape.

Given his hand — Solemnly confirming the oath.

Verse 20

20 And I will spread my net upon him, and he shall be taken in my snare, and I will bring him to Babylon, and will plead with him there for his trespass that he hath trespassed against me.

Plead — I will punish him.

Verse 21

21 And all his fugitives with all his bands shall fall by the sword, and they that remain shall be scattered toward all winds: and ye shall know that I the LORD have spoken it.

All — Not strictly, but the greatest part.

Verse 22

22 Thus saith the Lord GOD; I will also take of the highest branch of the high cedar, and will set it; I will crop off from the top of his young twigs a tender one, and will plant it upon an high mountain and eminent:

The highest branch — Of the royal seed; of the highest branch that is heir to the throne; namely, the Messiah.

An high mountain — Upon mount Zion.

Eminent — Not for outward splendor, but for spiritual advantages.

Verse 23

23 In the mountain of the height of Israel will I plant it: and it shall bring forth boughs, and bear fruit, and be a goodly cedar: and under it shall dwell all fowl of every wing; in the shadow of the branches thereof shall they dwell.

In the mountain — In Jerusalem.

All fowl — All nations.

In the shadow — There they shall find peace and safety.

Verse 24

24 And all the trees of the field shall know that I the LORD have brought down the high tree, have exalted the low tree, have dried up the green tree, and have made the dry tree to flourish: I the LORD have spoken and have done it.

The trees — The great ones on earth.

The high tree — The kingdom of Babylon, which was brought low indeed, when overthrown by Darius and Cyrus.

Chapter Eighteen

God reproves a corrupt proverb, ver. 1 - 4.
It shall be well with the righteous, ver. 5 - 9.
But ill with the wicked man, tho' he had a good father, ver. 10 - 13.
It shall be well with a good man, tho' he had a wicked father, ver. 14 - 18.
Therefore God is righteous, ver. 19 - 20.
It shall be well with penitents, but ill with apostates, ver. 21 - 29.
An exhortation to repentance, ver. 30 - 32.

Verse 2

2 What mean ye, that ye use this proverb concerning the land of Israel, saying, The fathers have eaten sour grapes, and the children's teeth are set on edge?

The land of Israel — The two tribes, not the ten.

The fathers — Our fore-fathers.

Have eaten — Have sinned.

The childrens — We their children, who were unborn, suffer for their sins.

Verse 4

4 Behold, all souls are mine; as the soul of the father, so also the soul of the son is mine: the soul that sinneth, it shall die.

Behold — There can be no colour of partial judgment in the proceedings of God, who is equally God to all.

All souls — All persons.

The soul — The person, whether father or son, shall die, shall bear his own punishment.

Verse 6

6 And hath not eaten upon the mountains, neither hath lifted up his eyes to the idols of the house of Israel, neither hath defiled his neighbour's wife, neither hath come near to a menstruous woman,

Hath not eaten — Hath not committed idolatry, offering sacrifice, and eating of the things sacrificed to idols; whose temples and altars were on mountains, Hosea 4:13.

Verse 8

8 He that hath not given forth upon usury, neither hath taken any increase, that hath withdrawn his hand from iniquity, hath executed true judgment between man and man,

Increase — Illegal interest.

Iniquity — Injustice of every kind.

Verse 9

9 Hath walked in my statutes, and hath kept my judgments, to deal truly; he is just, he shall surely live, saith the Lord GOD.

Shall live — Shall be delivered from famine, pestilence, and sword, and shall see good days.

Verse 13

13 Hath given forth upon usury, and

hath taken increase: shall he then live? he shall not live: he hath done all these abominations; he shall surely die; his blood shall be upon him.

His blood — Heb. 'Tis plural, bloods; both the blood of the innocent which he murdered, and his own blood which thereby he forfeited; the blood of his own soul and life: that is the whole blame of his misery in time and eternity, shall lie upon himself.

Verse 17

17 That hath taken off his hand from the poor, that hath not received usury nor increase, hath executed my judgments, hath walked in my statutes; he shall not die for the iniquity of his father, he shall surely live.

Hath taken off — Withdrawn his hand from hurting or wronging the poor, tho' he had power to do it securely.

Verse 20

20 The soul that sinneth, it shall die. The son shall not bear the iniquity of the father, neither shall the father bear the iniquity of the son: the righteousness of the righteous shall be upon him, and the wickedness of the wicked shall be upon him.

Shall not bear — This is a most unquestionable truth; and tho' perhaps it may seem otherwise in some cases, yet could we see perfectly the connexion between persons and persons; could we see the connexion of sins and sins, and how easily, secretly, and undiscerned men become guilty of the same sins, we should see father and son, though perhaps one of them might not do the evil, both guilty, and neither punished for the sin farther than if it was his own: nor do the scriptures, Exodus 20:5; Deuteronomy 28:18, doom persons to punishment for sins from which they are wholly free; but if children shall follow their fathers in sin, then if they die for those sins, 'tis because these are their own, not as they are their fathers.

The righteousness — It shall be well with the righteous, for he shall eat the fruit of his doing, he shall be rewarded as a righteous one.

The wickedness — The reward of wickedness. "The son shall not die, not die eternally, for the iniquity of the father, if he do not tread in the steps of it: nor the father for the iniquity of the son, if he do all he can to prevent it.

Verse 22

22 All his transgressions that he hath committed, they shall not be mentioned unto him: in his righteousness that he hath done he shall live.

Not mentioned — Not to him.

Verse 25

25 Yet ye say, The way of the Lord is not equal. Hear now, O house of Israel; Is not my way equal? are not your ways unequal?

The way — His whole management of affairs.

Not equal — Not right, or consistent with his own declaration, and law.

Verse 28

28 Because he considereth, and turneth away from all his transgressions that he hath committed, he shall surely live, he shall not die.

He shall surely live — "That is, he shall be restored to the favour of God, which is the life of the soul."

Verse 31

31 Cast away from you all your transgressions, whereby ye have transgressed; and make you a new heart and a new spirit: for why will ye die, O house of Israel?

Make you a new heart — Suffer me to do it in you.

Verse 32

32 For I have no pleasure in the death of him that dieth, saith the Lord GOD: wherefore turn yourselves, and live ye.

I have no pleasure — Sinners displease God when they undo themselves; they please him when they return.

Chapter Nineteen

The kingdom of Judah and house of David is compared to a lioness, and their princes to lions taken in nets, ver. 1 - 9.
The kingdom and house are compared to a vine, and these princes to branches, now broken off and burnt, ver. 10 - 14.

Verse 1

1 Moreover take thou up a lamentation for the princes of Israel,

For the princes — Jehoahaz, Jehoiachim, Jehoiachin, and Zedekiah.

Verse 2

2 And say, What is thy mother? A lioness: she lay down among lions, she nourished her whelps among young lions.

What — What resemblance shall I use to set out the nature, deportment, and state of the mother of these princes? Thy - One of whom was upon the throne at once, and therefore the prophet speaks to one at a time.

Mother — The land of Judea, and Jerusalem, the chief city of it, the royal family of David.

Lioness — Tho' chosen of God to execute justice; yet they soon degenerated into the fierce and ravening nature of the lioness.

Lay down — Associated, and grew familiar with neighbour kings, called here lions; fierce and bloody.

Her whelps — Her sons, successors to the crown.

Young lions — Either foreign princes and kings, or some of the fierce, unjust, tyrannizing princes at home.

Verse 3

3 And she brought up one of her whelps: it became a young lion, and it learned to catch the prey; it devoured men.

Brought up — Advanced, caused him to take the throne after the slaughter of Josiah.

One — Jehoahaz the second son of Josiah.

Became — Soon shewed his fierce, cruel, and bloody disposition.

Verse 4

4 The nations also heard of him; he was taken in their pit, and they brought him with chains unto the land of Egypt.

The nations — The Egyptians heard

what he did.

Verse 5

5 Now when she saw that she had waited, and her hope was lost, then she took another of her whelps, and made him a young lion.

Made him — King, and infused the lion-like maxims into him.

Verse 6

6 And he went up and down among the lions, he became a young lion, and learned to catch the prey, and devoured men.

He — Jehoiachim.

Went up — He continued eleven years on the throne; whereas Jehoahaz was taken as soon as he first ventured out.

The lions — Heathen kings, with whom he entered into leagues.

He became — Fierce, ravenous, unsatiable.

Verse 7

7 And he knew their desolate palaces, and he laid waste their cities; and the land was desolate, and the fulness thereof, by the noise of his roaring.

He knew — By taking them, he came to know their places, which are here called, what he made them, desolate.

Roaring — By the perpetual violent threats of this cruel king.

Verse 8

8 Then the nations set against him on every side from the provinces, and spread their net over him: he was taken in their pit.

The nations — Which were tributary to Nebuchadnezzar.

Set against — By order of the king of Babylon.

The provinces — Which belonged to the Babylonish kingdom.

Verse 10

10 Thy mother is like a vine in thy blood, planted by the waters: she was fruitful and full of branches by reason of many waters.

Thy mother — O thou prince of Israel.

By the waters — In a very fruitful soil.

Full of branches — Full of children; when Josiah died, he left four behind him, beside other branches of the royal line.

Verse 11

11 And she had strong rods for the sceptres of them that bare rule, and her stature was exalted among the thick branches, and she appeared in her height with the multitude of her branches.

Strong rods — Many excellent persons endowed with qualifications befitting kings, that they might sway the scepter.

Exalted — Above the ordinary majesty of other kingdoms.

Thick branches — This kingdom equalled, if not excelled, the greatest neighbour-kingdoms, and her kings exceeded all their neighbouring kings, in riches and power.

Verse 12

12 But she was plucked up in fury, she was cast down to the ground, and the east wind dried up her fruit: her strong rods were broken and withered; the fire consumed them.

The east wind — God raised up the king of Babylon to pull up this sinful kingdom.

Dried up — Blasted all her fruit, deposed her king, captivated him, his family, and the whole kingdom.

Strong rods — All the choice men.

Verse 13

13 And now she is planted in the wilderness, in a dry and thirsty ground.

She — A few of the branches of the last pruning.

In the wilderness — Tho' Babylon was in a very fruitful place, yet the cruelty of the Babylonians, made it to the Jews as terrible as a wilderness.

Verse 14

14 And fire is gone out of a rod of her branches, which hath devoured her fruit, so that she hath no strong rod to be a sceptre to rule. This is a lamentation, and shall be for a lamentation.

Fire — The fire of rebellion, kindled by Zedekiah, who is of the blood-royal.

No strong rod — The regal dignity is ceased.

Chapter Twenty

The prophet consulted by the elders, signifies God's displeasure against them, ver. 1 - 3.
Gives them a history of God's dealings with their fathers, and their treacherous dealings with God in Egypt, ver. 4 - 9.
In the wilderness, ver. 10 - 26.
In Canaan, ver. 27 - 32.
Judgments denounced against them, ver. 33 - 36.
Mercy promised to a remnant, ver. 37 - 44.
A word dropt toward Jerusalem, ver. 45 - 49.

Verse 1

1 And it came to pass in the seventh year, in the fifth month, the tenth day of the month, that certain of the elders of Israel came to enquire of the LORD, and sat before me.

The seventh year — Of Zedekiah's reign, two years and five months before Nebuchadnezzar besieged Jerusalem.

Came — Yet resolved before-hand what they would do.

Verse 3

3 Son of man, speak unto the elders of Israel, and say unto them, Thus saith the Lord GOD; Are ye come to enquire of me? As I live, saith the Lord GOD, I will not be enquired of by you.

Are ye come — Are ye in good earnest?

Verse 4

4 Wilt thou judge them, son of man, wilt thou judge them? cause them to know the abominations of their fathers:

Wilt thou — Wilt thou not convince and reprove them? And denounce my judgments against them? The abominations - What their fathers have done, they approve, and have outdone; by that let them know what to expect.

Verse 5

5 And say unto them, Thus saith the Lord GOD; In the day when I chose Israel, and lifted up mine hand unto the seed of the house of Jacob, and made myself known unto them in the land of Egypt, when I lifted up mine hand unto them, saying, I am the LORD your God;

When I chose — When I shewed that I had chosen them. The history of the rebellions of the children of Israel, begins as early, as their beginning. So does the history of man's apostasy from his Maker. No sooner have we read the story of his creation, but we meet with that of his rebellion. So we see here, it was with Israel; a people designed to represent the body of mankind, both in their dealings with God, and in God's dealing with them.

Lifted up my hand — Or stretched out and made bare my arm; that is, magnified my power for their deliverance.

When I lifted up mine hand — Shewed my power in performing my oath, and assuring them of doing what was farther promised.

Verse 6

6 In the day that I lifted up mine hand unto them, to bring them forth of the land of Egypt into a land that I had espied for them, flowing with milk and honey, which is the glory of all lands:

I had espied — God speaks after the manner of men.

Milk and honey — Literally milk and honey in abundance were in the land of Canaan. Proverbially it speaks the plenty and abundance of all the blessings of life.

Verse 7

7 Then said I unto them, Cast ye away every man the abominations of his eyes, and defile not yourselves with the idols of Egypt: I am the LORD your God.

Of his eyes — To which you have looked for help.

Verse 8

8 But they rebelled against me, and would not hearken unto me: they did not every man cast away the abominations of their eyes, neither did they forsake the idols of Egypt: then I said, I will pour out my fury upon them, to accomplish my anger against them in the midst of the land of Egypt.

To accomplish — To make an end of them.

Verse 9

9 But I wrought for my name's sake, that it should not be polluted before the heathen, among whom they were, in whose sight I made myself known unto them, in bringing them forth out of the land of Egypt.

For my name's sake — For the glory of my mercy and faithfulness.

Polluted — Reproached and blasphemed.

Verse 12

12 Moreover also I gave them my sabbaths, to be a sign between me and them, that they might know that I am the LORD that sanctify them.

A sign — Of their being peculiarly my people.

Verse 13

13 But the house of Israel rebelled against me in the wilderness: they walked not in my statutes, and they despised my judgments, which if a man do, he shall even live in them; and my sabbaths they greatly polluted: then I said, I would pour out my fury upon them in the wilderness, to consume them.

In the wilderness — Where they most needed my care and favour; where the preserving their life from destruction by the noxious creatures, and from famine by the barrenness of the wilderness, was a continued miracle.

Verse 15

15 Yet also I lifted up my hand unto them in the wilderness, that I would not bring them into the land which I had given them, flowing with milk and honey, which is the glory of all lands;

I lifted up my hand — I sware.

Them — So all the murmuring, disobedient, unbelieving generation was excluded, and their children were brought in.

Verse 18

18 But I said unto their children in the wilderness, Walk ye not in the statutes of your fathers, neither observe their judgments, nor defile yourselves with their idols:

Walk ye not — Live not as your fathers did.

Verse 20

20 And hallow my sabbaths; and they shall be a sign between me and you, that ye may know that I am the LORD your God.

Hallow — Remember to keep them holy.

Verse 22

22 Nevertheless I withdrew mine hand, and wrought for my name's sake, that it should not be polluted in the sight of the heathen, in whose sight I brought them forth.

I withdrew — God seems to take the posture of one that was just going to smite, yet draws back that he might spare.

Verse 23

23 I lifted up mine hand unto them also in the wilderness, that I would scatter them among the heathen, and disperse them through the countries;

I lifted — I sware.

Verse 25

25 Wherefore I gave them also statutes that were not good, and judgments whereby they should not live;

Wherefore — Because they rejected my good laws and judgments.

I gave them — Not by enjoining, but by permitting them to make such for themselves.

Not good — That were pernicious to the users.

Verse 26

26 And I polluted them in their own gifts, in that they caused to pass through the fire all that openeth the womb, that I might make them desolate, to the end that they might know that I am the LORD.

Polluted — I permitted them to pollute themselves.

Might know — Be forced to own, that the Lord is a mighty king in punishing those that would not have him a gracious king in governing them.

Verse 29

29 Then I said unto them, What is the high place whereunto ye go? And the name thereof is called Bamah unto this day.

What — What mean you that you go to the high place? What do you find so inviting there, that you will leave God's altar, where he requires your attendance, to frequent such places as he has forbidden you to worship in? Bamah - That is, the high place.

Verse 31

31 For when ye offer your gifts, when ye make your sons to pass through the fire, ye pollute yourselves with all your idols, even unto this day: and shall I be enquired of by you, O house of Israel? As I live, saith the Lord GOD, I will not be enquired of by you.

Shall I be enquired of — Are you fit to ask counsel of me, whom you have so obstinately forsaken and reproached?

Verse 32

32 And that which cometh into your mind shall not be at all, that ye say, We will be as the heathen, as the families of the countries, to serve wood and stone.

And that — God to convince them, tells them what they think and have purposed.

Shall not be — Shall be quite frustrated.

We will be — Will unite with them in marriages, commerce, and religion too; and then we shall be safe among them.

Verse 34

34 And I will bring you out from the people, and will gather you out of the countries wherein ye are scattered, with a mighty hand, and with a stretched out arm, and with fury poured out.

The people — Sidonians, Ammonites, Moabites, or whoever they were, to whom the apostate Jews betook themselves, where they thought to lurk, God will bring them thence into Babylonish captivity.

Verse 35

35 And I will bring you into the wilderness of the people, and there will I plead with you face to face.

Bring you — Drive you.

The wilderness — Into the most horrid parts of the world; into the mountainous parts of Media, Hyrcania, Iberia, Caspia, Albania, and Scythia.

Plead with you — Pass sentence, and execute it on you.

Verse 36

36 Like as I pleaded with your fathers

in the wilderness of the land of Egypt, so will I plead with you, saith the Lord GOD.

Your fathers — Who died there, and never entered Canaan.

Verse 37

37 And I will cause you to pass under the rod, and I will bring you into the bond of the covenant:

I will cause — I will bring you out by number, so that you shall either own my scepter, or by a conquered subjection, yield to my sword and power.

Under the rod — Referring to the manner of shepherds in that country, who did tell their sheep in, and out of the fold.

Bring you — The voluntary and obedient into covenant with myself.

Verse 38

38 And I will purge out from among you the rebels, and them that transgress against me: I will bring them forth out of the country where they sojourn, and they shall not enter into the land of Israel: and ye shall know that I am the LORD.

The rebels — The stubborn sinners.

Verse 39

39 As for you, O house of Israel, thus saith the Lord GOD; Go ye, serve ye every one his idols, and hereafter also, if ye will not hearken unto me: but pollute ye my holy name no more with your gifts, and with your idols.

But pollute — But while ye are such idolaters, forbear to take my name into your lips.

Verse 40

40 For in mine holy mountain, in the mountain of the height of Israel, saith the Lord GOD, there shall all the house of Israel, all of them in the land, serve me: there will I accept them, and there will I require your offerings, and the firstfruits of your oblations, with all your holy things.

Mine holy mountain — Sion, God's holy hill, Psalms 2:6. Holy by designation, and God's own appointing it for his temple and presence.

Of the height — Sion, tho' lower than many other hills, yet was above them all for God's peculiar presence.

In the land — Their own land.

Your offerings — When I have brought you into the land, then I will require your offerings as formerly: you shall see my temple built, Jerusalem filled with inhabitants, and my worship restored.

Verse 41

41 I will accept you with your sweet savour, when I bring you out from the people, and gather you out of the countries wherein ye have been scattered; and I will be sanctified in you before the heathen.

Sanctified — Magnified and praised for the good I do to my people.

Verse 43

43 And there shall ye remember your ways, and all your doings, wherein ye have been defiled; and ye shall lothe yourselves in your own sight for all your evils that ye have committed.

Remember — Review your former ways with sorrow: remember, and grieve.

Verse 46

46 Son of man, set thy face toward the south, and drop thy word toward the south, and prophesy against the forest of the south field;

The south — Look toward Jerusalem, and the land of Canaan.

Drop thy word — Let thy word distil, begin with softer words, before thou shower down with the vehemency of a storm.

The forest — Jerusalem, which was become like a forest.

Verse 47

47 And say to the forest of the south, Hear the word of the LORD; Thus saith the Lord GOD; Behold, I will kindle a fire in thee, and it shall devour every green tree in thee, and every dry tree: the flaming flame shall not be quenched, and all faces from the south to the north shall be burned therein.

Every green tree — All that flourish, and all that are poor.

All faces — All persons and orders of men, from one end of the land to the other.

Verse 49

49 Then said I, Ah Lord GOD! they say of me, Doth he not speak parables?

Parables — So absolutely, that we cannot understand him.

Chapter Twenty-One

An explication of the prophecy in the close of the last chapter, with directions to the prophet upon it, ver. 1 - 7.
A prediction of the sword that was coming on the land, ver. 8 - 17.
A prospect given of the king of Babylon's coming to Jerusalem, to which he was determined by divination, ver. 18 - 24.
Sentence passed on Zedekiah, ver. 25 - 27.
The destruction of the Ammonites, ver. 28 - 32.

Verse 2

2 Son of man, set thy face toward Jerusalem, and drop thy word toward the holy places, and prophesy against the land of Israel,

The holy places — The temple and all parts of it.

Verse 3

3 And say to the land of Israel, Thus saith the LORD; Behold, I am against thee, and will draw forth my sword out of his sheath, and will cut off from thee the righteous and the wicked.

The righteous — It is no unusual thing, that in publick calamities, those who are indeed righteous should be involved with others.

Verse 4

4 Seeing then that I will cut off from thee the righteous and the wicked, therefore shall my sword go forth out of his sheath against all flesh from the south to the north:

All flesh — All the Jews that dwell in the land.

Verse 5

5 That all flesh may know that I the LORD have drawn forth my sword out of his sheath: it shall not return any more.

Shall not return — It shall not return into the scabbard 'till it hath done full execution.

Verse 6

6 Sigh therefore, thou son of man, with the breaking of thy loins; and with bitterness sigh before their eyes.

Sigh therefore — Thereby express deep sorrow.

Breaking of thy loins — Like a woman in travail.

Verse 7

7 And it shall be, when they say unto thee, Wherefore sighest thou? that thou shalt answer, For the tidings; because it cometh: and every heart shall melt, and all hands shall be feeble, and every spirit shall faint, and all knees shall be weak as water: behold, it cometh, and shall be brought to pass, saith the Lord GOD.

Because — The saddest news you ever heard is coming.

Verse 9

9 Son of man, prophesy, and say, Thus saith the LORD; Say, A sword, a sword is sharpened, and also furbished:

Furbished — Made clean and bright.

Verse 10

10 It is sharpened to make a sore slaughter; it is furbished that it may glitter: should we then make mirth? it contemneth the rod of my son, as every tree.

Of my son — To whom God saith, Thou shalt break them with a rod of iron, Psalms 2:9. This sword is that rod of iron, which despiseth every tree, and will bear it down.

Verse 12

12 Cry and howl, son of man: for it shall be upon my people, it shall be upon all the princes of Israel: terrors by reason of the sword shall be upon my people: smite therefore upon thy thigh.

It — The devouring sword.

Upon thy thigh — In token of thy sense of what they must suffer.

Verse 13

13 Because it is a trial, and what if the sword contemn even the rod? it shall be no more, saith the Lord GOD.

If — But if the king and kingdom of Judah despise this trial, both shall be destroyed and be no more.

Verse 14

14 Thou therefore, son of man, prophesy, and smite thine hands together, and let the sword be doubled the third time, the sword of the slain: it is the sword of the great men that are slain, which entereth into their privy chambers.

And smite — In token of amazement and sorrow.

Of the slain — Wherewith many shall be slain.

Privy chambers — Where they were hidden in hope to escape.

Verse 15

15 I have set the point of the sword against all their gates, that their heart may faint, and their ruins be multiplied: ah! it is made bright, it is wrapped up for the slaughter.

All their gates — Both of cities, of palaces, and of private houses.

Wrapt up — And hath been carefully kept in the scabbard, that it might not be blunted.

Verse 16

16 Go thee one way or other, either on the right hand, or on the left, whithersoever thy face is set.

Go — O sword, take thy own course.

Verse 17

17 I will also smite mine hands together, and I will cause my fury to rest: I the LORD have said it.

Smite my hands — In token of my approbation.

Verse 19

19 Also, thou son of man, appoint thee two ways, that the sword of the king of Babylon may come: both twain shall come forth out of one land: and choose thou a place, choose it at the head of the way to the city.

Appoint — Paint, or describe them on a tile.

One land — That is, Babylon.

Chuse — Pitch on some convenient place, where thou mayest place Nebuchadnezzar's army, consulting where this one way divides into two, which was on the edge of the desert of Arabia.

At the head — Where each way runs, toward either Rabbath, or Jerusalem; for there Nebuchadnezzar will cast lots.

Verse 20

20 Appoint a way, that the sword may come to Rabbath of the Ammonites, and to Judah in Jerusalem the defenced.

To Judah — The Jews.

Verse 21

21 For the king of Babylon stood at the parting of the way, at the head of the two ways, to use divination: he made his arrows bright, he consulted with images, he looked in the liver.

Stood — The prophet speaks of what shall be, as if it were already.

To use — To consult with his gods, and to cast lots.

Arrows — Writing on them the names of the cities, then putting them into a quiver, and thence drawing them out and concluding, according to the name which was drawn.

He consulted — Perhaps by a divine permission, the devil gave them answers from those images.

In the liver — They judged of future events, by the entrails, and more especially by the liver.

Verse 22

22 At his right hand was the divination

for Jerusalem, to appoint captains, to open the mouth in the slaughter, to lift up the voice with shouting, to appoint battering rams against the gates, to cast a mount, and to build a fort.

The divination — The divination which concerned Jerusalem, was managed on his right hand.

Verse 23

23 And it shall be unto them as a false divination in their sight, to them that have sworn oaths: but he will call to remembrance the iniquity, that they may be taken.

Them — The Jews.

That have sworn — Zedekiah, his princes, and nobles, who swore allegiance to the king of Babylon, these perjured persons will contemn all predictions of the prophet.

He — Nebuchadnezzar.

The iniquity — The wickedness of their perjury and rebellion.

They — Zedekiah, and the Jews with him

Verse 24

24 Therefore thus saith the Lord GOD; Because ye have made your iniquity to be remembered, in that your transgressions are discovered, so that in all your doings your sins do appear; because, I say, that ye are come to remembrance, ye shall be taken with the hand.

Your transgressions — Against God, and against the king of Babylon.

Discovered — To all in court, city, and country.

With the hand — As birds, or beasts in the net, are taken with the hands, so shall you, and be carried into Babylon.

Verse 25

25 And thou, profane wicked prince of Israel, whose day is come, when iniquity shall have an end,

And thou — Zedekiah.

Whose day — The day of sorrows, and sufferings, and punishment is at hand.

Shall have an end — Shall bring the ruin of king and kingdom, and with the overthrow of your state, the means of sinning shall end too.

Verse 26

26 Thus saith the Lord GOD; Remove the diadem, and take off the crown: this shall not be the same: exalt him that is low, and abase him that is high.

The diadem — The royal attire of the head, which the king daily wore.

Shall not be the same — The kingdom shall never be what it hath been.

Him that is low — Jeconiah. The advance of this captive king, came to pass in the thirty-seventh year of his captivity.

Verse 27

27 I will overturn, overturn, overturn, it: and it shall be no more, until he come whose right it is; and I will give it him.

Shall be no more — Never recover its former glory, 'till the scepter be quite taken away from Judah, and way be made for the Messiah. He hath an incontestable right to the dominion both in the church and in the world. And in due time he shall have the possession of it, all adverse power being overturned.

Verse 28

28 And thou, son of man, prophesy and say, Thus saith the Lord GOD concerning the Ammonites, and concerning their reproach; even say thou, The sword, the sword is drawn: for the slaughter it is furbished, to consume because of the glittering:

Their reproach — Wherewith they reproached Israel in the day of Israel's afflictions.

Verse 29

29 Whiles they see vanity unto thee, whiles they divine a lie unto thee, to bring thee upon the necks of them that are slain, of the wicked, whose day is come, when their iniquity shall have an end.

While — While thy astrologers, and soothsayers, deceive thee with fair, but false divinations.

To bring thee — To bring thee under the sword of the Chaldeans, and destroy thee as the Jews; to make thee stumble and fall on their necks, as men that fall among a multitude of slain.

Verse 30

30 Shall I cause it to return into his sheath? I will judge thee in the place where thou wast created, in the land of thy nativity.

Shall I cause it — God will by no means suffer the sword to be sheathed.

Judge thee — Condemn, and execute.

Verse 31

31 And I will pour out mine indignation upon thee, I will blow against thee in the fire of my wrath, and deliver thee into the hand of brutish men, and skilful to destroy.

I will blow — As those who melt down metals blow upon the metal in the fire, that the fire may burn the fiercer.

Chapter Twenty-Two

A catalogue of the sins of Jerusalem, ver. 1 - 12.
Punishment threatened, ver. 13 - 16.
They are condemned as dross to the fire, ver. 17 - 22.
All orders of men having contributed to the national guilt, must share in the punishment of it, ver. 23 - 31.

Verse 2

2 Now, thou son of man, wilt thou judge, wilt thou judge the bloody city? yea, thou shalt shew her all her abominations.

Judge — The question is doubled, to awaken the prophet more fully, and to quicken him to his work.

Verse 3

3 Then say thou, Thus saith the Lord GOD, The city sheddeth blood in the midst of it, that her time may come, and maketh idols against herself to defile herself.

Her time — The time of ripeness in her sins, and of execution of judgments on her.

To defile — For this does more defile them, and provoke God to wrath against them.

Verse 4

4 Thou art become guilty in thy blood that thou hast shed; and hast defiled thyself in thine idols which thou hast made; and thou hast caused thy days to draw near, and art come even unto thy years: therefore have I made thee a reproach unto the heathen, and a mocking to all countries.

Thy days — The days of thy sorrows, and punishment.

Art come — Thou art grown up to the eldest years in sin, beyond which thou art not to go.

Verse 5

5 Those that be near, and those that be far from thee, shall mock thee, which art infamous and much vexed.

Much vexed — Afflicted, impoverished, and ruined.

Verse 6

6 Behold, the princes of Israel, every one were in thee to their power to shed blood.

Every one — Not one to be found of a more merciful temper.

To their power — According to their ability.

Verse 7

7 In thee have they set light by father and mother: in the midst of thee have they dealt by oppression with the stranger: in thee have they vexed the fatherless and the widow.

In thee — In Jerusalem.

Verse 8

8 Thou hast despised mine holy things, and hast profaned my sabbaths.

Thou — O Jerusalem.

Mine holy things — All mine institutions, temple, sacrifices, feasts.

Verse 9

9 In thee are men that carry tales to shed blood: and in thee they eat upon the mountains: in the midst of thee they commit lewdness.

Carry tales — Informers, or persons that for money, give in false witness against the innocent.

They eat — Offer sacrifice on the mountains and feast there, in honour of their idols.

Verse 10

10 In thee have they discovered their fathers' nakedness: in thee have they humbled her that was set apart for pollution.

Discovered — Defiled their fathers bed.

Verse 13

13 Behold, therefore I have smitten mine hand at thy dishonest gain which thou hast made, and at thy blood which hath been in the midst of thee.

Smitten mine hand — In testimony of my abhorrence.

Verse 14

14 Can thine heart endure, or can thine hands be strong, in the days that I shall deal with thee? I the LORD have spoken it, and will do it.

Endure — Withstand the evils that are coming, or bear them when come.

Verse 16

16 And thou shalt take thine inheritance in thyself in the sight of the heathen, and thou shalt know that I am the LORD.

In thyself — Whereas I was thine inheritance so long as thou wert a holy, obedient people; now be an inheritance to thyself, if thou canst.

Verse 18

18 Son of man, the house of Israel is to me become dross: all they are brass, and tin, and iron, and lead, in the midst of the furnace; they are even the dross of silver.

Dross — Utterly degenerate, and base metal.

The furnace — The afflictions I have laid upon them have not bettered them.

The dross — While they loved mercy, did justly, walked humbly with their God, they were as silver; now they are but dross.

Verse 19

19 Therefore thus saith the Lord GOD; Because ye are all become dross, behold, therefore I will gather you into the midst of Jerusalem.

Gather you — From all parts. I will, by a secret over-ruling providence, bring you into Jerusalem, as into a furnace, where you may be consumed.

Verse 23

23 And the word of the LORD came unto me, saying,

Her — The land of Israel.

Not cleansed — Though God's judgments have been as violent floods; and as hottest fires.

Nor rained upon — Yet neither thy filth hath been carried away, nor thy dross melted out of thee. Therefore thou shalt be deprived of the rain, that should cool thy thirsty land.

Verse 25

25 There is a conspiracy of her prophets in the midst thereof, like a roaring lion ravening the prey; they have devoured souls; they have taken the treasure and precious things; they have made her many widows in the midst thereof.

A conspiracy — A contrivance, to speak all alike, smooth words, and give out promises of peace and safety.

Thereof — Of the land.

The treasure — As a reward of their lies.

Made her — By persuading Zedekiah to hold out the war, which filled Jerusalem with dead husbands, and forlorn widows.

Verse 26

26 Her priests have violated my law, and have profaned mine holy things: they have put no difference between the holy and profane, neither have they shewed difference between the unclean and the clean, and have hid their eyes from my sabbaths, and I am profaned among them.

My holy things — Sacrifices, and oblations.

Put no difference — Neither have they in their practice, differenced holy and profane, nor in their teaching acquainted the people with the difference, nor in the exercise of their authority, separated the profane from the holy, either persons, or things.

Hid their eyes — Despised, and would not see the holiness of the sabbaths.

Profaned — Contemned, dishonoured, disobeyed.

Verse 27

27 Her princes in the midst thereof are like wolves ravening the prey, to shed blood, and to destroy souls, to get dishonest gain.

Destroy souls — Ruin families; cutting off the fathers, and impoverishing the widow, and fatherless.

Verse 28

28 And her prophets have daubed them with untempered morter, seeing vanity, and divining lies unto them, saying, Thus saith the Lord GOD, when the LORD hath not spoken.

Daubed them — Flattered them, in their ways of sin.

Untempered mortar — With promises that like ill-tempered mortar, will deceive them, though all seems at present smooth and safe.

Verse 30

30 And I sought for a man among them, that should make up the hedge, and stand in the gap before me for the land, that I should not destroy it: but I found none.

I sought — God speaks after the manner of men.

A man — Any one, among princes, prophets, priests, or people, to repair the breach.

And stand — Interpose between a sinful people, and their offended God, and intreat for mercy.

But — All were corrupted.

Chapter Twenty-Three

The apostacy of Israel and Samaria from God, ver. 1 - 8.
Their ruin, ver. 9, 10.
The apostacy of Judah and Jerusalem from God, ver. 11 - 21.
Their ruin, ver. 22 - 35.
The joint wickedness of them both, ver. 36 - 44.
And their joint ruin, ver. 45 - 49.

Verse 2

2 Son of man, there were two women, the daughters of one mother:

Two women — Judah, and Israel, two kingdoms.

Verse 3

3 And they committed whoredoms in Egypt; they committed whoredoms in their youth: there were their breasts pressed, and there they bruised the teats of their virginity.

Whoredoms — Idolatry.

Verse 4

4 And the names of them were Aholah

the elder, and Aholibah her sister: and they were mine, and they bare sons and daughters. Thus were their names; Samaria is Aholah, and Jerusalem Aholibah.

Aholah — That is, his own tabernacle; for Israel falling off from the house of David, fell off from the tabernacle, or temple of God; so that all the temple they had was of their own making.

The elder — Greater for number of tribes, and for power, wealth, and for multitudes of people.

Aholibah — That is, my tabernacle in her: the two tribes had the temple of God with them.

Mine — By solemn marriage-covenant.

Bare sons — Were fruitful and brought forth children to me; they increased in numbers of people; and among these, some there were that were children of God by faith, love, and obedience.

Verse 5

5 And Aholah played the harlot when she was mine; and she doted on her lovers, on the Assyrians her neighbours,

Played the harlot — United in idolatry, with the Assyrians.

Mine — When under my government, and protection.

Verse 6

6 Which were clothed with blue, captains and rulers, all of them desirable young men, horsemen riding upon horses.

Horsemen — Skillful in riding, and well furnished with choice horses.

Verse 7

7 Thus she committed her whoredoms with them, with all them that were the chosen men of Assyria, and with all on whom she doted: with all their idols she defiled herself.

With all — Other nations, with whom she had commerce.

Verse 10

10 These discovered her nakedness: they took her sons and her daughters, and slew her with the sword: and she became famous among women; for they had executed judgment upon her.

Discovered — Stript her naked, and exposed her to shame.

Took her sons — Captives.

Slew her — The kingdom of Israel, under Hoshea, was by Salmanesar utterly destroyed.

They — The Assyrians, had executed God's just displeasure upon her.

Verse 15

15 Girded with girdles upon their loins, exceeding in dyed attire upon their heads, all of them princes to look to, after the manner of the Babylonians of Chaldea, the land of their nativity:

Girded — With soldiers belts, which includes the rest of the habit of soldiers.

In dyed attire — Both rich, comely, large, and of divers colours.

Princes — Of princely aspect and majesty.

Verse 17

17 And the Babylonians came to her into the bed of love, and they defiled her with their whoredom, and she was polluted with them, and her mind was alienated from them.

Alienated — She grew weary of the Chaldeans.

Verse 18

18 So she discovered her whoredoms, and discovered her nakedness: then my mind was alienated from her, like as my mind was alienated from her sister.

Discovered — Made it appear to all, far and near.

Verse 19

19 Yet she multiplied her whoredoms, in calling to remembrance the days of her youth, wherein she had played the harlot in the land of Egypt.

By — Remembering her idolatries in Egypt, her alliance with it in days past, which she now resolved to act over again.

Verse 20

20 For she doted upon their paramours, whose flesh is as the flesh of asses, and whose issue is like the issue of horses.

Paramours — The nations, that were confederate with the Egyptians.

Verse 23

23 The Babylonians, and all the Chaldeans, Pekod, and Shoa, and Koa, and all the Assyrians with them: all of them desirable young men, captains and rulers, great lords and renowned,

all of them riding upon horses.

Pekod — Pekod is the province between Tigris, and Lycus; in this was old Nineveh.

Shoa — Either Sia in Armenia, or the Sohia, among which were the Adiabeni, and this contained the middle part of the kingdom of Babylon.

Koa — This bordered upon Media, the inhabitants were called Kohai, and dwelt about Arbela.

And all — All subjects of the Assyrian monarchy.

Verse 24

24 And they shall come against thee with chariots, wagons, and wheels, and with an assembly of people, which shall set against thee buckler and shield and helmet round about: and I will set judgment before them, and they shall judge thee according to their judgments.

And wheels — Lest in their march the carriage wheels should break, a store of these were provided.

An assembly — A mighty confluence of people.

I will set — Give them a power in right of conquest over their rebels, as well as mine, and I will give them a spirit of judgment to discern the greatness of this people's sins.

Judge — Condemn, and execute sentence upon thee.

According — To their will, power, wrath, and custom, against rebels; for these are their rules of judgment.

Verse 25

25 And I will set my jealousy against thee, and they shall deal furiously with thee: they shall take away thy nose and thine ears; and thy remnant shall fall by the sword: they shall take thy sons and thy daughters; and thy residue shall be devoured by the fire.

I will set my jealousy — As a jealous provoked husband, I will be as much against thee as they are.

Thy residue — Either the people, who hid themselves in vaults and cellars, or what the Chaldeans cannot carry away, all this shall be devoured by fire.

Verse 29

29 And they shall deal with thee hatefully, and shall take away all thy labour, and shall leave thee naked and bare: and the nakedness of thy whoredoms shall be discovered, both thy lewdness and thy whoredoms.

Take away — Deprive thee of the comfortable use of all thy labour, which they will exact of thee in captivity.

Verse 32

32 Thus saith the Lord GOD; Thou shalt drink of thy sister's cup deep and large: thou shalt be laughed to scorn and had in derision; it containeth much.

It — Is large, and contains what will last many years, even 'till the seventy years be expired.

Verse 34

34 Thou shalt even drink it and suck it out, and thou shalt break the sherds thereof, and pluck off thine own breasts: for I have spoken it, saith the Lord GOD.

Thou — Shalt stagger with sorrows, that shall intoxicate, and astonish.

Suck it out — The dregs shalt thou drink, and multiply thine own sorrows.

Break the sheards — To suck out what remains.

And pluck — Revenging thyself upon thyself.

Verse 35

35 Therefore thus saith the Lord GOD; Because thou hast forgotten me, and cast me behind thy back, therefore bear thou also thy lewdness and thy whoredoms.

Bear thou — The guilt, I will impute it, the punishment, I will not pardon it.

Verse 38

38 Moreover this they have done unto me: they have defiled my sanctuary in the same day, and have profaned my sabbaths.

In the same day — When they had newly polluted themselves with idolatry and murder, they thrust into the temple.

Verse 39

39 For when they had slain their children to their idols, then they came the same day into my sanctuary to profane it; and, lo, thus have they done in the midst of mine house.

My house — Nay, these things have been in my house.

Verse 40

40 And furthermore, that ye have sent for men to come from far, unto whom a messenger was sent; and, lo, they came: for whom thou didst wash thyself, paintedst thy eyes, and deckedst thyself with ornaments,

Wash thyself — After the manner of harlots.

Verse 41

41 And satest upon a stately bed, and a table prepared before it, whereupon thou hast set mine incense and mine oil.

Sattest — Prepared to feast them.

A stately bed — A magnificent bed, on which women sat to feast, when men leaned on their sides.

Incense — Offered to their idols.

Verse 42

42 And a voice of a multitude being at ease was with her: and with the men of the common sort were brought Sabeans from the wilderness, which put bracelets upon their hands, and beautiful crowns upon their heads.

A voice — A shout for joy, that there was a treaty of peace between the Jews, and the Chaldeans.

Verse 45

45 And the righteous men, they shall judge them after the manner of adulteresses, and after the manner of women that shed blood; because they are adulteresses, and blood is in their hands.

Righteous men — Men that keep the law of their God.

Verse 46

46 For thus saith the Lord GOD; I will bring up a company upon them, and will give them to be removed and spoiled.

Upon them — Against the Jews, the children of this Aholibah.

Verse 47

47 And the company shall stone them with stones, and dispatch them with their swords; they shall slay their sons and their daughters, and burn up their houses with fire.

The company — The Babylonian army.

Verse 48

48 Thus will I cause lewdness to cease out of the land, that all women may be taught not to do after your lewdness.

Lewdness — Idolatry. And indeed we do not read of any after their return out of this captivity.

Verse 49

49 And they shall recompense your lewdness upon you, and ye shall bear the sins of your idols: and ye shall know that I am the Lord GOD.

They — The Babylonians.

The sins — The guilt of worshipping idols; and you shall bear the punishment of idolaters.

Chapter Twenty-Four

By the sign of flesh boiling in a pot are shewed, the miseries of Jerusalem during the siege, ver. 1 - 14.

By the sign of Ezekiel's not mourning for his wife is shewed, that the approaching calamities would be to great to be lamented, ver. 15 - 27.

Verse 1

1 Again in the ninth year, in the tenth month, in the tenth day of the month, the word of the LORD came unto me, saying,

In the ninth year — Of Zedekiah's reign.

Came unto me — The prophet was now in Babylon.

Verse 2

2 Son of man, write thee the name of the day, even of this same day: the king of Babylon set himself against Jerusalem this same day.

Set himself — Sat down to besiege.

Verse 4

4 Gather the pieces thereof into it, even every good piece, the thigh, and the shoulder; fill it with the choice bones.

Every good piece — All the chief of the inhabitants of the land, the wealthiest, who will fly from their country-houses to live in safety in Jerusalem: the most war-like, who will betake themselves to Jerusalem for its defence.

Fill it — With those pieces that are biggest, fullest of marrow, and which are divided according to the bones; these are the principal members of the state, the king, princes, priests, magistrates, and the most wealthy citizens.

Verse 5

5 Take the choice of the flock, and burn also the bones under it, and make it boil well, and let them seethe the bones of it therein.

The bones — Not of the pieces to be boiled, but of the many innocents murdered in Jerusalem; for their blood crieth for vengeance, and their bones scattered on the face of the earth, will both make and maintain this fire.

Verse 6

6 Wherefore thus saith the Lord GOD; Woe to the bloody city, to the pot whose scum is therein, and whose scum is not gone out of it! bring it out piece by piece; let no lot fall upon it.

The bloody city — Jerusalem.

Whose scum — Her wickedness is still within her.

Piece by piece — One piece after another 'till all be consumed.

No lot — Lots are for saving some, but here shall be no sparing any.

Verse 7

7 For her blood is in the midst of her; she set it upon the top of a rock; she poured it not upon the ground, to cover it with dust;

The blood — Innocent blood which she hath shed.

The top of a rock — Where it might be long seen.

To cover it — These butchers of innocent ones leave their blood uncovered.

Verse 8

8 That it might cause fury to come up to take vengeance; I have set her blood upon the top of a rock, that it should not be covered.

I have set — I will openly punish, and in such a manner as shall not be soon forgotten.

Verse 10

10 Heap on wood, kindle the fire, consume the flesh, and spice it well, and let the bones be burned.

And spice it well — To express this justice, that is acceptable to God and men.

The bones — The greatest, strongest, and firmest of the Jews shall perish in this fiery indignation.

Verse 11

11 Then set it empty upon the coals thereof, that the brass of it may be hot, and may burn, and that the filthiness of it may be molten in it, that the scum of it may be consumed.

The filthiness — A type of the unreformed sinfulness of the city.

Molten — That their wickedness may be taken away with their persons, and city.

Verse 12

12 She hath wearied herself with lies, and her great scum went not forth out of her: her scum shall be in the fire.

She — Jerusalem.

With lies — Her allies, their promises, their forces, and their idols, all prove a lie to the house of Judah.

Her scum — Her unrepented sins shall be punished in the fire that burns their city.

Verse 13

13 In thy filthiness is lewdness: because I have purged thee, and thou wast not purged, thou shalt not be purged from thy filthiness any more, till I have caused my fury to rest upon thee.

Lewdness — Or obstinacy and boldness.

Purged thee — Used all means to purge thee.

Verse 16

16 Son of man, behold, I take away from thee the desire of thine eyes with a stroke: yet neither shalt thou mourn nor weep, neither shall thy tears run down.

With a stroke — A sudden stroke, by my own immediate hand. We know not how soon the desire of our eyes may be removed from us. Death is a stroke, which the most pious, the most useful, the most amiable are not exempted from.

Verse 17

17 Forbear to cry, make no mourning for the dead, bind the tire of thine head upon thee, and put on thy shoes upon thy feet, and cover not thy lips, and eat not the bread of men.

Bind the tire — Adorn thy head, as thou wast used to do; go not bare-headed as a mourner.

Thy shoes — In great mournings the

Jews went bare-footed.

Cover not thy lips — It was a custom among them to cover the upper lip.

Eat not — Of thy neighbours and friends, who were wont to visit their mourning friends, and send in choice provision to their houses.

Verse 18

18 So I spake unto the people in the morning: and at even my wife died; and I did in the morning as I was commanded.

I spake — Told them what I expected would be.

Verse 21

21 Speak unto the house of Israel, Thus saith the Lord GOD; Behold, I will profane my sanctuary, the excellency of your strength, the desire of your eyes, and that which your soul pitieth; and your sons and your daughters whom ye have left shall fall by the sword.

Profane — Cast off, and put into the hands of Heathens.

The excellency of your strength — So it was while God's presence was there.

The desire — As much your desire, as my wife was mine; most dear to you.

Verse 22

22 And ye shall do as I have done: ye shall not cover your lips, nor eat the bread of men.

Ye shall do — When you are in captivity, where you may not use your own customs.

Verse 23

23 And your tires shall be upon your heads, and your shoes upon your feet: ye shall not mourn nor weep; but ye shall pine away for your iniquities, and mourn one toward another.

Pine away — You shall languish with secret sorrow, when you shall not dare to shew it openly.

Verse 25

25 Also, thou son of man, shall it not be in the day when I take from them their strength, the joy of their glory, the desire of their eyes, and that whereupon they set their minds, their sons and their daughters,

Their strength — Their walls and fortifications.

The joy — All their public and private joys and hopes shall be destroyed in the destruction of the kingdom, and their children.

Verse 26

26 That he that escapeth in that day shall come unto thee, to cause thee to hear it with thine ears?

To hear it — To give thee a narrative of all he had seen.

Verse 27

27 In that day shall thy mouth be opened to him which is escaped, and thou shalt speak, and be no more dumb: and thou shalt be a sign unto them; and they shall know that I am the LORD.

No more dumb — From this prophecy for eighteen months during the siege, he does not prophesy of Israel, but of other nations.

Thou shalt be a sign — Until the event shall convince the Jews, thou shalt by sign, signify to them, what is coming.

Chapter Twenty-Five

A prophesy against the Ammonites, ver. 1 - 7.
The Moabites, ver. 8 - 11.
The Edomites, ver. 12 - 14.
And the Philistines, ver. 15 - 17.

Verse 3

3 And say unto the Ammonites, Hear the word of the Lord GOD; Thus saith the Lord GOD; Because thou saidst, Aha, against my sanctuary, when it was profaned; and against the land of Israel, when it was desolate; and against the house of Judah, when they went into captivity;

Aha — When thou shouldest have pitied, thou didst proudly insult over my people.

Verse 4

4 Behold, therefore I will deliver thee to the men of the east for a possession, and they shall set their palaces in thee, and make their dwellings in thee: they shall eat thy fruit, and they shall drink thy milk.

The men of the east — The Arabians, associates of Nebuchadnezzar, who recompensed their service, with giving them this country when it was conquered, as it was five years after the desolation of Jerusalem.

Verse 5

5 And I will make Rabbah a stable for camels, and the Ammonites a couchingplace for flocks: and ye shall know that I am the LORD.

Rabbah — The royal city, called since Philadelphia from the king of Egypt who built it.

The Ammonites — The land they dwelt in.

Verse 7

7 Behold, therefore I will stretch out mine hand upon thee, and will deliver thee for a spoil to the heathen; and I will cut thee off from the people, and I will cause thee to perish out of the countries: I will destroy thee; and thou shalt know that I am the LORD.

Know — Thus God will bring those that were strangers to him into an acquaintance with him, and it will be a blessed effect of their calamities. How much better is it, to be poor and know God, than to be rich, and ignorant of him?

Verse 8

8 Thus saith the Lord GOD; Because that Moab and Seir do say, Behold, the house of Judah is like unto all the heathen;

Seir — The seed of Esau, the Edomites. Seir was the mountain where they first planted themselves.

Is like — Are no more a select people than others.

Verse 9

9 Therefore, behold, I will open the side of Moab from the cities, from his cities which are on his frontiers, the glory of the country, Bethjeshimoth, Baalmeon, and Kiriathaim,

The side — That part of his country

which was best fortified.

Bethjeshimoth — An ancient city; it was a fortress toward the desert, which watched lest any should make an inroad on the country.

Verse 10

10 Unto the men of the east with the Ammonites, and will give them in possession, that the Ammonites may not be remembered among the nations.

With the Ammonites — As I have given Ammon, so I will with them give Moab to the Chaldeans, who will give it to the Arabians.

Verse 13

13 Therefore thus saith the Lord GOD; I will also stretch out mine hand upon Edom, and will cut off man and beast from it; and I will make it desolate from Teman; and they of Dedan shall fall by the sword.

Teman — A country in the southern coast of Edom.

Dedan — Adjoining to Edom.

Verse 15

15 Thus saith the Lord GOD; Because the Philistines have dealt by revenge, and have taken vengeance with a despiteful heart, to destroy it for the old hatred;

It — Israel.

Verse 16

16 Therefore thus saith the Lord GOD; Behold, I will stretch out mine hand upon the Philistines, and I will cut off the Cherethims, and destroy the remnant of the sea coast.

The Cherethim — The bowmen, the strength of Philistia.

The remnant — Who had escaped the sword of Samuel, David, Hezekiah, and of Psammetichus king of Egypt.

Chapter Twenty-Six

The sin of Tyre, ver. 1, 2.
The utter destruction of it, ver. 3 - 14.
The astonishment of the neighbouring nations, ver. 15 - 21.

Verse 1

1 And it came to pass in the eleventh year, in the first day of the month, that the word of the LORD came unto me, saying,

In the eleventh year — Of Jechoniah's captivity, the year wherein Jerusalem was taken.

The month — That month which followed the taking of Jerusalem.

Verse 2

2 Son of man, because that Tyrus hath said against Jerusalem, Aha, she is broken that was the gates of the people: she is turned unto me: I shall be replenished, now she is laid waste:

Because — Probably God revealed this to the prophet as soon as these insulting Tyrians spoke it.

The gates — The great mart of nations, people from all parts.

She is turned — The trading interest will turn to me.

Verse 4

4 And they shall destroy the walls of Tyrus, and break down her towers: I will also scrape her dust from her, and make her like the top of a rock.

Scrape — I will leave thee nothing; thou shalt be scraped, and swept, that not so much as dust shall remain in thee.

Like — As bare as was the rock on which thy city is built.

Verse 6

6 And her daughters which are in the field shall be slain by the sword; and they shall know that I am the LORD.

Her daughters — The lesser cities.

In the field — On the firm land.

Verse 11

11 With the hoofs of his horses shall he tread down all thy streets: he shall slay thy people by the sword, and thy strong garrisons shall go down to the ground.

Garrisons — Bastions, or forts, or triumphal arches.

Verse 12

12 And they shall make a spoil of thy riches, and make a prey of thy merchandise: and they shall break down thy walls, and destroy thy pleasant houses: and they shall lay thy stones and thy timber and thy dust in the midst of the water.

Shall lay — It had been a quicker way, to have burnt all; but the greedy soldier might dream of treasures hid in walls, or under the timber, and therefore take the pains to pull all down, and throw it into the sea.

Verse 14

14 And I will make thee like the top of a rock: thou shalt be a place to spread nets upon; thou shalt be built no more: for I the LORD have spoken it, saith the Lord GOD.

No more — Tho' there was a city of that name built, yet it was built on the continent; and in propriety of speech, was another city.

Verse 15

15 Thus saith the Lord GOD to Tyrus; Shall not the isles shake at the sound of thy fall, when the wounded cry, when the slaughter is made in the midst of thee?

The isles — Isles which are places freest from danger of invasions, will shake with fear, when they learn that Tyre is fallen.

Verse 16

16 Then all the princes of the sea shall come down from their thrones, and lay away their robes, and put off their broidered garments: they shall clothe themselves with trembling; they shall sit upon the ground, and shall tremble at every moment, and be astonished at thee.

The princes — Who were lords of the islands of that sea.

Come down — In token of condolence.

Trembling — They shall be afraid of their own concerns, and astonished in the midst of their fears.

Verse 18

18 Now shall the isles tremble in the day of thy fall; yea, the isles that are in the sea shall be troubled at thy departure.

In the sea — At a great distance, and farther from land.

Departure — Leaving thy ancient dwelling, to go into captivity.

Verse 19

19 For thus saith the Lord GOD; When I shall make thee a desolate city, like the cities that are not inhabited; when I shall bring up the deep upon thee, and great waters shall cover thee;

The deep — Nebuchadnezzar's army.

Great waters — Great afflictions.

Verse 20

20 When I shall bring thee down with them that descend into the pit, with the people of old time, and shall set thee in the low parts of the earth, in places desolate of old, with them that go down to the pit, that thou be not inhabited; and I shall set glory in the land of the living;

Bring thee down — When I shall slay thee, and throw thee into the grave.

With the people — Who are long since dead, and gone to eternity.

The low parts — Another description of the grave, from the situation and solitude of it.

Set glory — Then I will restore the beauty, strength, and wealth of Israel, and bring them back to Jerusalem.

In the land — In the land of Judea, called, land of the living, because a land, where God will bless, and give life by his word, ordinances, and spirit: thus different shall Tyre's captivity and Jerusalem's be.

Verse 21

21 I will make thee a terror, and thou shalt be no more: though thou be sought for, yet shalt thou never be found again, saith the Lord GOD.

A terror — To all that hear of thee.

Chapter Twenty-Seven

A large account of the wealth, splendor and trade of Tyre, ver. 1 - 25.
Its utter ruin, and the consternation of its neighbours, ver. 26 - 36.

Verse 2

2 Now, thou son of man, take up a lamentation for Tyrus;

A lamentation — We ought to mourn for the miseries of other nations, as well as of our own, out of an affection for mankind in general; yea, tho' they have brought them upon themselves.

Verse 3

3 And say unto Tyrus, O thou that art situate at the entry of the sea, which art a merchant of the people for many isles, Thus saith the Lord GOD; O Tyrus, thou hast said, I am of perfect beauty.

At the entry — Heb. Entrances. She was about four furlongs, or half an English mile from the continent, as it were in the very door of the sea.

Verse 5

5 They have made all thy ship boards of fir trees of Senir: they have taken cedars from Lebanon to make masts for thee.

They — The shipwrights.

Shipboards — The planks and benches, or transoms for their ships.

Fir-trees — Of the best and finest fir-trees.

Lebanon — Whose cedars excelled others.

Verse 6

6 Of the oaks of Bashan have they made thine oars; the company of the Ashurites have made thy benches of ivory, brought out of the isles of Chittim.

With box — From the isles, and parts about the Ionian, Aegean, and other seas of the Mediterranean, where box-tree is a native, and of great growth and firmness, fit to saw into boards for benches; they were conveyed to Tyre, where their artists inlaid these box boards with ivory, and made them beautiful seats in their ships.

Verse 7

7 Fine linen with broidered work from Egypt was that which thou spreadest forth to be thy sail; blue and purple from the isles of Elishah was that which covered thee.

The isles of Elishah — Probably the sea-coast of Aeolis in the lesser Asia, the inhabitants whereof were excellent in the skill of dying wool.

Which covered — He speaks of the coverings they used in their ships or galleys: their tilts, as our boat-men call them.

Verse 8

8 The inhabitants of Zidon and Arvad were thy mariners: thy wise men, O Tyrus, that were in thee, were thy pilots.

Zidon — An ancient town and haven of Phoenicia, not far from Tyre.

Arvad — Or Aradus, an island belonging to Phoenicia, twenty furlongs from the continent.

Mariners — Rowers in thy galleys; the rich Tyrians would not employ their own in such servile works, they hired strangers.

Wise men — Thy learned men: for navigation was the great study of the Tyrians.

Verse 9

9 The ancients of Gebal and the wise men thereof were in thee thy calkers: all the ships of the sea with their mariners were in thee to occupy thy merchandise.

The ancients — Old experienced workmen.

Gebal — A town of Phoenicia near the sea.

The wise men — Skilful in their trades.

Were in thee — Who dwelt in Tyre for gain.

All the ships — Ships from all parts of the sea, full of mariners, not only to manage the ships at sea, but to offer their service to the Tyrians for bringing in, or carrying out their wares.

Verse 10

10 They of Persia and of Lud and of Phut were in thine army, thy men of war: they hanged the shield and helmet in thee; they set forth thy comeliness.

Lud — Lydians, not those Cresus was king over, but those that dwelt in Egypt about the lake Maraeolis.

Phut — Lybians, a people of Africa; these were their hired soldiers.

Hanged the shield — In time of peace.

They set forth — These stout, expert, well armed guards, were an honour to thee.

Verse 11

11 The men of Arvad with thine army were upon thy walls round about, and the Gammadims were in thy towers: they hanged their shields upon thy walls round about; they have made thy beauty perfect.

With — Mixed with other hired soldiers.

The Gammadim — Probably men of Gammade, a town of Phoenicia.

Verse 13

13 Javan, Tubal, and Meshech, they were thy merchants: they traded the persons of men and vessels of brass in thy market.

Javan — The Grecians, particularly the Ionians.

Tubal — The Asiatic Iberians, and the Albanians toward the Caspian sea.

Meshech — The Cappadocians.

They traded — Brought men to sell for slaves.

Verse 14

14 They of the house of Togarmah traded in thy fairs with horses and horsemen and mules.

Of the house — Of the country.

Togarmah — Armenia the lesser, Phrygia, Galatia, or Cappadocia.

Horsemen — It is likely they might sell grooms, as best able to manage, and keep those horses.

Verse 15

15 The men of Dedan were thy merchants; many isles were the merchandise of thine hand: they brought thee for a present horns of ivory and ebony.

Isles — In the Indian seas, and in the Red-sea traded with thee.

Horns — Elk's horns, or wild goats.

Ebony — Is a very solid, heavy, shining, black wood, fit for many choice works.

Verse 16

16 Syria was thy merchant by reason of the multitude of the wares of thy making: they occupied in thy fairs with emeralds, purple, and broidered work, and fine linen, and coral, and agate.

The multitude — The abundance of the Tyrian manufactures.

Verse 17

17 Judah, and the land of Israel, they were thy merchants: they traded in thy market wheat of Minnith, and Pannag, and honey, and oil, and balm.

Minnith — The name of an excellent wheat country.

Pannag — Some obscure place, which now is forgotten.

Verse 19

19 Dan also and Javan going to and fro occupied in thy fairs: bright iron, cassia, and calamus, were in thy market.

Javan — In the isle of Meroe, in Egypt.

Verse 20

20 Dedan was thy merchant in precious clothes for chariots.

Dedan — The posterity of Abraham by Keturah, who dwelt in Arabia, and were sheep-masters.

Clothes — With which they lined their chariots.

Verse 22

22 The merchants of Sheba and Raamah, they were thy merchants: they occupied in thy fairs with chief of all spices, and with all precious stones, and gold.

Sheba — A country in Arabia Felix.

Raamah — Another people of the same Arabia.

Verse 23

23 Haran, and Canneh, and Eden, the merchants of Sheba, Asshur, and Chilmad, were thy merchants.

Haran — In Mesopotamia, where Abraham dwelt.

Canneh — This is supposed to be the same with Calneh, Genesis 10:10, afterwards Ctesiphon, a pleasant city on Tigris.

Ashur — Assyria.

Chilmad — A country between Assyria and Parthia.

Verse 25

25 The ships of Tarshish did sing of thee in thy market: and thou wast replenished, and made very glorious in the midst of the seas.

The ships — The ships from all parts of the sea.

Did sing — Had their songs to commend thy state.

Verse 26

26 Thy rowers have brought thee into great waters: the east wind hath broken thee in the midst of the seas.

Thy rowers — Thy governors and counsellors.

Great waters — Dangers and difficulties.

The east wind — The king of Babylon with his army.

Hath broken — As surely will, as if he had already done it.

In the midst — Where thou thoughtest thyself impregnable.

Verse 27

27 Thy riches, and thy fairs, thy merchandise, thy mariners, and thy pilots, thy calkers, and the occupiers of thy merchandise, and all thy men of war, that are in thee, and in all thy company which is in the midst of thee, shall fall into the midst of the seas in the day of thy ruin.

All thy company — All that are men fit for war, in the multitudes of people that are in thee.

Shall fall — These all shall fall together.

Verse 28

28 The suburbs shall shake at the sound of the cry of thy pilots.

The suburbs — The suburbs, which are nearest the sea, shall first hear the outcries of pilots, and mariners.

Verse 29

29 And all that handle the oar, the mariners, and all the pilots of the sea, shall come down from their ships, they shall stand upon the land;

Shall come down — In the allegory of a miserable shipwreck, the prophet sets forth the fall of Tyre; and in this verse he represents them all shifting out of the sinking ship, in great confusion.

Verse 30

30 And shall cause their voice to be heard against thee, and shall cry bitterly, and shall cast up dust upon their heads, they shall wallow themselves in the ashes:

Wallow themselves in ashes — As men use to do in their greatest mournings.

Verse 32

32 And in their wailing they shall take up a lamentation for thee, and lament over thee, saying, What city is like Tyrus, like the destroyed in the midst of the sea?

In the sea — Alas! what was once her safeguard, is now her grave.

Verse 33

33 When thy wares went forth out of the seas, thou filledst many people; thou didst enrich the kings of the earth with the multitude of thy riches and of thy merchandise.

Went forth — Were landed.

Thou filledst — There was enough to supply to the full.

Verse 34

34 In the time when thou shalt be broken by the seas in the depths of the waters thy merchandise and all thy company in the midst of thee shall fall.

By the seas — The Babylonians, that like seas shall swell, roar, and break in upon thee.

Verse 35

35 All the inhabitants of the isles shall be astonished at thee, and their kings shall be sore afraid, they shall be troubled in their countenance.

Troubled — They shall not be able to conceal the discomposure of their mind, but will shew it in their countenance.

Verse 36

36 The merchants among the people shall hiss at thee; thou shalt be a terror, and never shalt be any more.

Shall hiss — Will mock at thy fall.

Chapter Twenty-Eight

A prediction of the ruin of the king of Tyre, ver. 1 - 10.
A lamentation for him, ver. 11 - 19.
A prediction of the destruction of Zidon, ver. 20 - 23.
The restoration of Israel, ver. 24 - 26.

Verse 2

2 Son of man, say unto the prince of Tyrus, Thus saith the Lord GOD; Because thine heart is lifted up, and thou hast said, I am a God, I sit in the seat of God, in the midst of the seas; yet thou art a man, and not God, though thou set thine heart as the heart of God:

Hast said — In thy heart.

In the seat of God — Safe and impregnable as heaven itself.

A man — Subject to casualties, sorrows, and distresses.

Set thine heart — Thou hast entertained thoughts, which become none but God.

Verse 3

3 Behold, thou art wiser than Daniel; there is no secret that they can hide from thee:

Wiser — In thy own thoughts.

Daniel — Who was then famous for his wisdom.

Verse 7

7 Behold, therefore I will bring strangers upon thee, the terrible of the nations: and they shall draw their swords against the beauty of thy wisdom, and they shall defile thy brightness.

The beauty — Those beautiful things, in which thy wisdom appeared.

Verse 10

10 Thou shalt die the deaths of the uncircumcised by the hand of strangers: for I have spoken it, saith the Lord GOD.

The deaths — Temporal and eternal.

Of the uncircumcised — Of the wicked, an accursed death.

Verse 12

12 Son of man, take up a lamentation upon the king of Tyrus, and say unto him, Thus saith the Lord GOD; Thou sealest up the sum, full of wisdom, and perfect in beauty.

Thou sealest up — Thou fanciest that fulness of wisdom, and perfection of beauty are in thee.

Verse 13

13 Thou hast been in Eden the garden of God; every precious stone was thy covering, the sardius, topaz, and the diamond, the beryl, the onyx, and the jasper, the sapphire, the emerald, and the carbuncle, and gold: the workmanship of thy tabrets and of thy pipes was prepared in thee in the day that thou wast created.

In Eden — In the midst of all delights.

The workmanship — Now the prophet notes their joys, musick, and songs, both to loud, and to softer musick, as the lute, and tabret in the day of their kings coronation, and all this on instruments of most exquisite make, and of their own artists work; in this they exceeded as in the other.

Created — King: in the day of thy coronation.

Verse 14

14 Thou art the anointed cherub that covereth; and I have set thee so: thou wast upon the holy mountain of God; thou hast walked up and down in the midst of the stones of fire.

Cherub — For thy wisdom, power, and excellency, like a cherub, or angel; for the sacredness of thy person, and office, as the anointed of God; for the exercise of thy power, as a shield, as a protector of the weak.

And I — I, whom thou forgetest have made thee so.

Thou wast — Thou wast advanced to kingly dignity, (which David calls a mountain, Psalms 30:7,) a sacred office, and of divine institution.

In the midst — Surrounded with stones, that sparkle like fire.

Verse 15

15 Thou wast perfect in thy ways from the day that thou wast created, till iniquity was found in thee.

Thou wast perfect — Is not this an irony?

Verse 16

16 By the multitude of thy merchandise they have filled the midst of thee with violence, and thou hast sinned: therefore I will cast thee as profane out of the mountain of God: and I will destroy thee, O covering cherub, from the midst of the stones of fire.

I will cast — Out thy kingly dignity.

Verse 17

17 Thine heart was lifted up because of thy beauty, thou hast corrupted thy wisdom by reason of thy brightness: I will cast thee to the ground, I will lay thee before kings, that they may behold thee.

Corrupted — Depraved, or lost thy wisdom.

Behold thee — That thou mayst be a spectacle, and warning to them.

Verse 18

18 Thou hast defiled thy sanctuaries by the multitude of thine iniquities, by the iniquity of thy traffick; therefore will I bring forth a fire from the midst of thee, it shall devour thee, and I will bring thee to ashes upon the earth in the sight of all them that behold thee.

I will bring thee — Thou shalt be burnt to ashes, and trampled under feet.

Verse 19

19 All they that know thee among the people shall be astonished at thee: thou shalt be a terror, and never shalt thou be any more.

All — All that have formerly known thy riches, power, allies, and wisdom.

Verse 22

22 And say, Thus saith the Lord GOD; Behold, I am against thee, O Zidon; and I will be glorified in the midst of thee: and they shall know that I am the LORD, when I shall have executed judgments in her, and shall be sanctified in her.

Zidon — A city, north-west from Canaan, a king's seat of old, and from which Tyre descended.

I will be glorified — When my judgments make my justice, power and truth appear, both you, and others shall confess my glory.

Sanctified — Owned as holy, reverenced as just, obeyed as sovereign.

Verse 23

23 For I will send into her pestilence, and blood into her streets; and the wounded shall be judged in the midst of her by the sword upon her on every side; and they shall know that I am the LORD.

And blood — Bloody war by an enemy, that shall bring the war to the gates, nay into the streets of Zidon.

Judged — Be punished in the midst of the city.

The sword — By the sword of her enemies.

Verse 24

24 And there shall be no more a pricking brier unto the house of Israel, nor any grieving thorn of all that are round about them, that despised them; and they shall know that I am the Lord GOD.

A pricking briar — By these two metaphors the prophet points out the troublesome neighbours of the Jews, such as Moab, Ammon, Edom, Tyre, and Zidon. This never had a full accomplishment yet. But it will, for the scripture cannot be broken.

Verse 25

25 Thus saith the Lord GOD; When I shall have gathered the house of Israel from the people among whom they are scattered, and shall be sanctified in them in the sight of the heathen, then shall they dwell in their land that I have given to my servant Jacob.

Sanctified — I was dishonoured by the Jews in the sight of the heathen, and I will be honoured by the Jews in their sight.

Chapter Twenty-Nine

A prediction of the destruction of Pharaoh, for his treacherous dealing with Israel, ver. 1 - 7.
A prediction of the desolation of Egypt, ver. 8 - 12.
A promise of the restoration thereof in part, ver. 13 - 16.
A prediction of Nebuchadrezzar's passing it, ver. 17 - 20.
A promise of mercy to Israel, ver. 21.

Verse 1

1 In the tenth year, in the tenth month, in the twelfth day of the month, the word of the LORD came unto me, saying,

The tenth year — Of Jeconiah's captivity.

Verse 3

3 Speak, and say, Thus saith the Lord GOD; Behold, I am against thee, Pharaoh king of Egypt, the great dragon that lieth in the midst of his rivers, which hath said, My river is mine own, and I have made it for myself.

The great dragon — The crocodile; our prophet, as well as Isaiah, compares the

Egyptian king to that devouring serpent, or dragon.

That lieth — Not only at rest, but waiting for prey.

My river — My kingdom, power, riches, and forces, all the strength and glory of Egypt.

Verse 4

4 But I will put hooks in thy jaws, and I will cause the fish of thy rivers to stick unto thy scales, and I will bring thee up out of the midst of thy rivers, and all the fish of thy rivers shall stick unto thy scales.

Put hooks — The Allegory is continued.

The fish — The people of Egypt.

To stick — To adhere to their king.

Verse 5

5 And I will leave thee thrown into the wilderness, thee and all the fish of thy rivers: thou shalt fall upon the open fields; thou shalt not be brought together, nor gathered: I have given thee for meat to the beasts of the field and to the fowls of the heaven.

Leave thee — When thus brought out, I will leave thee.

The wilderness — The deserts of Libya and Syene.

All the fish — The whole army of the Egyptians.

The open fields — There was this king and his army ruined.

Gathered — These were not buried, but left in the wilderness, a prey to wild beasts, and birds.

Verse 7

7 When they took hold of thee by thy hand, thou didst break, and rend all their shoulder: and when they leaned upon thee, thou brakest, and madest all their loins to be at a stand.

Rent — Didst them much mischief instead of benefiting them, as thou hast promised, Jeremiah 37:7.

Verse 10

10 Behold, therefore I am against thee, and against thy rivers, and I will make the land of Egypt utterly waste and desolate, from the tower of Syene even unto the border of Ethiopia.

Syene — Boundary between Ethiopia and Egypt; that is, all Egypt from north-east to south-west.

Verse 11

11 No foot of man shall pass through it, nor foot of beast shall pass through it, neither shall it be inhabited forty years.

Forty years — These forty years began about the thirtieth year of Jeconiah's captivity, and end with the seventieth year of the captivity, which was the first of Cyrus.

Verse 14

14 And I will bring again the captivity of Egypt, and will cause them to return into the land of Pathros, into the land of their habitation; and they shall be there a base kingdom.

Pathros — The southern part of Egypt, in which was the famous city Thebae, known for its hundred gates.

Their habitation — The ancient habitation of their fathers.

A base — A low, tributary, dependent kingdom.

Verse 15

15 It shall be the basest of the kingdoms; neither shall it exalt itself any more above the nations: for I will diminish them, that they shall no more rule over the nations.

No more rule — Though in the times of the Ptolemeys, it was considerable, yet then, even then it did not rule the nations about her.

Verse 16

16 And it shall be no more the confidence of the house of Israel, which bringeth their iniquity to remembrance, when they shall look after them: but they shall know that I am the Lord GOD.

Which — Which sinful reliance on the arm of flesh provoked God to call to mind their other iniquities.

When — When they forgot God, and respected Egypt.

They — The house of Israel.

Verse 17

17 And it came to pass in the seven and twentieth year, in the first month, in the first day of the month, the word of the LORD came unto me, saying,

In the seven and twentieth year — Of Jeconiah's captivity, the year after the conquest of Tyre.

Verse 18

18 Son of man, Nebuchadrezzar king of Babylon caused his army to serve a great service against Tyrus: every head was made bald, and every shoulder was peeled: yet had he no wages, nor his army, for Tyrus, for the service that he had served against it:

Caused — The army, and commanders were weary of the siege, but the immovable resolution of the king kept them on.

A great service — It was service to the justice of God. It was great service both for hardness of work, heaviness of burdens, and length of the siege, thirteen years together.

Made bald — Through age, or sicknesses, or continued wearing of helmets.

Peeled — Galled with carrying burdens.

No wages — For though Tyre was very rich, when first besieged, much wealth was carried away during the siege, much spent and wasted in the siege, and what was left, preserved by articles of surrender.

Verse 19

19 Therefore thus saith the Lord GOD; Behold, I will give the land of Egypt unto Nebuchadrezzar king of Babylon; and he shall take her multitude, and take her spoil, and take her prey; and it shall be the wages for his army.

Her multitude — Common people, who shall be made captives, and servants or slaves.

Her prey — What she had before taken from others.

The wages — God will be behind-hand with none, who do any service for him; one way or other he will recompence them. None shall kindle a fire at his altar for nought.

Verse 20

20 I have given him the land of Egypt for his labour wherewith he served against it, because they wrought for me, saith the Lord GOD.

They — The Babylonians.

For me — God's work was doing by them, tho' they thought nothing less.

Verse 21

21 In that day will I cause the horn of the house of Israel to bud forth, and I will give thee the opening of the mouth in the midst of them; and they shall know that I am the LORD.

The horn — Jehoiakim, who was then advanced by Evil-Merodach.

The opening of the mouth — Thou shalt have liberty, to open thy mouth in comforting the good among them, and to give praise to God.

Chapter Thirty

The steps by which Nebuchadrezzar would destroy Egypt, ver. 1 - 19. A repetition of a former prophecy against it, ver. 20 - 26.

Verse 2

2 Son of man, prophesy and say, Thus saith the Lord GOD; Howl ye, Woe worth the day!

Ye — Inhabitants of Egypt.

Verse 3

3 For the day is near, even the day of the LORD is near, a cloudy day; it shall be the time of the heathen.

A cloudy day — So times of trouble are called.

Of the heathen — The time when God will reckon with the Heathens.

Verse 4

4 And the sword shall come upon Egypt, and great pain shall be in Ethiopia, when the slain shall fall in Egypt, and they shall take away her multitude, and her foundations shall be broken down.

Ethiopia — The neighbour and ally to Egypt.

Take away — Into miserable captivity.

Her foundations — Their government, laws, and strong holds.

Verse 5

5 Ethiopia, and Libya, and Lydia, and all the mingled people, and Chub, and the men of the land that is in league, shall fall with them by the sword.

Lydia — Not the Asiatic, but the Africans placed between some part of Cyrene and Egypt.

The mingled people — The hired soldiers from all parts, a confused mixture of nations.

And Chub — The inhabitants of the inmost Libya; perhaps they may be the Nubians at this day.

The men — All the allies of Egypt.

With them — With the Egyptians.

Verse 6

6 Thus saith the LORD; They also that uphold Egypt shall fall; and the pride of her power shall come down: from the tower of Syene shall they fall in it by the sword, saith the Lord GOD.

Upheld — Those that favour and help her.

The pride — The glory of all her strength.

Verse 7

7 And they shall be desolate in the midst of the countries that are desolate, and her cities shall be in the midst of the cities that are wasted.

They — All those before mentioned.

Verse 8

8 And they shall know that I am the LORD, when I have set a fire in Egypt, and when all her helpers shall be destroyed.

Destroyed — The fire that consumes nations is of God's kindling: and when he sets fire to a kingdom, all they that go about to quench the fire, shall be consumed by it.

Verse 9

9 In that day shall messengers go forth from me in ships to make the careless Ethiopians afraid, and great pain shall come upon them, as in the day of Egypt: for, lo, it cometh.

Messengers — Such as having escaped the sword, shall tell the news.

From me — By my permission and providence.

In ship's — Messengers by ships might carry the news to both the Ethiopian, Asian, and African, by the Red-sea.

As in the day — During the mighty havock made by the Chaldeans.

It — A like storm.

Verse 11

11 He and his people with him, the terrible of the nations, shall be brought to destroy the land: and they shall draw their swords against Egypt, and fill the land with the slain.

His people — His own subjects, not hired soldiers.

Verse 12

12 And I will make the rivers dry, and sell the land into the hand of the wicked: and I will make the land waste, and all that is therein, by the hand of strangers: I the LORD have spoken it.

The rivers dry — Probably the Chaldeans diverted them, and so their fortified towns wanted one great defence.

Sell — Give it up entirely.

Verse 13

13 Thus saith the Lord GOD; I will also destroy the idols, and I will cause their images to cease out of Noph; and there shall be no more a prince of the land of Egypt: and I will put a fear in the land of Egypt.

Noph — Memphis, now Grand Cairo, the chief city of the country.

A prince — Either an Egyptian born, or independent, and over all Egypt.

A fear — Consternation and cowardice.

Verse 14

14 And I will make Pathros desolate, and will set fire in Zoan, and will execute judgments in No.

In Zoan — Zoan shall be burnt down to ashes.

In No — A great and populous city situate on one of the mouths of the Nile.

Verse 15

15 And I will pour my fury upon Sin, the strength of Egypt; and I will cut off the multitude of No.

Sin — Pelusium, which was the key of Egypt, and therefore always well fortified, and strongly garrisoned.

Verse 16

16 And I will set fire in Egypt: Sin shall have great pain, and No shall be rent asunder, and Noph shall have distresses daily.

Shall be rent — Her walls, and towers, and fortresses broken through by the violence of engines, and by the assaults of the soldiers.

Verse 17

17 The young men of Aven and of Pibeseth shall fall by the sword: and these cities shall go into captivity.

Young men — 'Tis probable these might be a body of valiant youths, collected out of these ten cities.

Aven — Bethshemesh, or Heliopolis, an idolatrous city, in which was a stately temple of the sun: an hundred and fifty furlongs, that is six miles and three quarters in compass.

Phibeseth — Bubastus, sometimes called Hoephestus, not far from Aven.

Verse 18

18 At Tehaphnehes also the day shall be darkened, when I shall break there the yokes of Egypt: and the pomp of her strength shall cease in her: as for her, a cloud shall cover her, and her daughters shall go into captivity.

Tehaphnehes — A great and goodly city of Egypt; Tachapanes, Tachpanes, Tahapanes, Tahpanes, Chanes, and Hanes, are names given it, and this from a queen of Egypt of that name in Solomon's time. It stood not far from Sin, or Pelusium.

Darkened — A night shall come upon it.

Break — I shall break the kingdom of Egypt, that it no more oppress with yokes, that is, burdens.

Her daughters — Her towns and villages.

Verse 20

20 And it came to pass in the eleventh year, in the first month, in the seventh day of the month, that the word of the LORD came unto me, saying,

The eleventh year — Of Jeconiah's captivity, three months and two days before Jerusalem was taken, about the time that the Egyptians attempted to raise the siege of Jerusalem.

Verse 21

21 Son of man, I have broken the arm of Pharaoh king of Egypt; and, lo, it shall not be bound up to be healed, to put a roller to bind it, to make it strong to hold the sword.

Have broken — Partly by the victory of the Chaldeans over Pharaoh-necho, partly by the victory of the Cyreneans over Pharaoh-hophra.

The sword — None can heal the wounds that God gives but himself. They whom he disables, cannot again hold the sword.

Verse 22

22 Therefore thus saith the Lord GOD; Behold, I am against Pharaoh king of Egypt, and will break his arms, the strong, and that which was broken; and I will cause the sword to fall out of his hand.

His arms — Both his arms.

The strong — That part of his kingdom which remains entire.

Broken — That which was shattered before.

Verse 25

25 But I will strengthen the arms of the king of Babylon, and the arms of Pharaoh shall fall down; and they shall know that I am the LORD, when I shall put my sword into the hand of the king of Babylon, and he shall stretch it out upon the land of Egypt.

Will strengthen — As judges on the bench like Pilate, so generals in the field, like Nebuchadrezzar, have no power but what is given them from above.

Chapter Thirty-One

The greatness and power of the king of Assyria, ver. 1 - 9.
His security and destruction, ver. 10 - 17.
This applied to Pharaoh, ver. 18.

Verse 2

2 Son of man, speak unto Pharaoh king of Egypt, and to his multitude; Whom art thou like in thy greatness?

His multitude — His numerous subjects.

Verse 3

3 Behold, the Assyrian was a cedar in Lebanon with fair branches, and with a shadowing shroud, and of an high stature; and his top was among the thick boughs.

A cedar — Like the most goodly cedar for strength and beauty.

Verse 4

4 The waters made him great, the deep set him up on high with her rivers running round about his plants, and sent out her little rivers unto all the trees of the field.

The waters — Cedars grow great by the water-courses.

The deep — The sea sent out her waters, which gave being to the rivers, that watered him.

His plants — The provinces of this mighty kingdom, that were like plants about a great tree.

All the trees — To all his subjects.

Verse 5

5 Therefore his height was exalted above all the trees of the field, and his boughs were multiplied, and his branches became long because of the multitude of waters, when he shot forth.

All the fowls — All kind of men, nobles, merchants, husbandmen.

Made their nests — Settled their habitations.

In his boughs — In his kingdom, in the cities and towns of it.

All great nations — No nation that was great at that time, but, sought the friendship of this kingdom.

Verse 8

8 The cedars in the garden of God could not hide him: the fir trees were not like his boughs, and the chesnut trees were not like his branches; nor any tree in the garden of God was like unto him in his beauty.

The cedars — The greatest kings.

Garden of God — In the most fruitful gardens.

Hide — Could not ever top, and shade him.

The fir-trees — Lesser kings, and kingdoms, were not equal to his boughs.

Nor any tree — All summed up, none like him in all the kingdoms of the world.

Verse 11

11 I have therefore delivered him into the hand of the mighty one of the heathen; he shall surely deal with him: I have driven him out for his wickedness.

Him — The proud king of Assyria, Sardanapalus.

The mighty one — Arbaces, who first struck at the root of this Cedar, might well be styled the mighty one of the heathen, since he could bring together four hundred thousand of Medes, Persians, Babylonians, and Arabians.

Verse 12

12 And strangers, the terrible of the nations, have cut him off, and have left him: upon the mountains and in all the valleys his branches are fallen, and his boughs are broken by all the rivers of the land; and all the people of the earth are gone down from his shadow, and have left him.

Strangers — Foreigners.

Verse 14

14 To the end that none of all the trees by the waters exalt themselves for their height, neither shoot up their top among the thick boughs, neither their trees stand up in their height, all that drink water: for they are all delivered unto death, to the nether parts of the earth, in the midst of the children of men, with them that go down to the pit.

To the end — All this is designed to be a warning to mortals.

All the trees — The emperors, kings, or flourishing states.

By the waters — Planted most commodiously, and furnished most abundantly with power and wealth.

The children of men — As common men, of no quality or distinction.

Verse 15

15 Thus saith the Lord GOD; In the day when he went down to the grave I caused a mourning: I covered the deep for him, and I restrained the floods thereof, and the great waters were stayed: and I caused Lebanon to mourn for him, and all the trees of the field fainted for him.

He — The king of Assyria.

A mourning — There was much lamentation.

Fainted — Probably there were portentous signs in the sea, and great waters, and the rivers, and among the trees.

Verse 16

16 I made the nations to shake at the sound of his fall, when I cast him down to hell with them that descend into the pit: and all the trees of Eden, the choice and best of Lebanon, all that drink water, shall be comforted in the nether parts of the earth.

Shake — All that heard the noise of his fall, trembled at it.

Cast him down — Brought the king and kingdom, as a dead man to the grave among them, that before were dead and buried.

All the trees — All kings, and particularly the greatest.

All that drink water — Enjoyed great power, riches, and glory.

Comforted — He speaks to the dead with allusion to the manner of the living, who rejoice to see the proud brought low.

Verse 17

17 They also went down into hell with him unto them that be slain with the sword; and they that were his arm, that dwelt under his shadow in the midst of the heathen.

They also — His neighbouring kings.

Hell — Perished with him, and went to those whom God had slain for their pride and wickedness.

They that were his arm — His loyal and faithful subjects and friends, on whom he relied, and by whom he acted.

Verse 18

18 To whom art thou thus like in glory and in greatness among the trees of Eden? yet shalt thou be brought down with the trees of Eden unto the nether parts of the earth: thou shalt lie in the midst of the uncircumcised with them that be slain by the sword. This is Pharaoh and all his multitude, saith the Lord GOD.

Yet — Thou shalt be like them in thy fall.

Thou shalt lie — As unclean, despised, loathsome and under a curse.

This is — This will be their end.

Chapter Thirty-Two

The destruction of Egypt is represented under the similitude of killing a lion and a crocodile, ver. 1 - 16.
Under that of the funeral of a great general, ver. 17 - 30.

Verse 1

1 And it came to pass in the twelfth year, in the twelfth month, in the first day of the month, that the word of the LORD came unto me, saying,

Twelfth year — Of the captivity of Jeconiah.

Verse 2

2 Son of man, take up a lamentation for Pharaoh king of Egypt, and say unto him, Thou art like a young lion of the nations, and thou art as a whale in the seas: and thou camest forth with thy rivers, and troubledst the waters with thy feet, and fouledst their rivers.

Like a young lion — Spoiling all thou canst.

Crocodile — The crocodiles lay in the rivers, though sometimes they went down the river to the sea.

With thy rivers — Raisedst mighty armies, and didst lead them out against thy neighbours.

The waters — The people, and kings near thee.

Thy feet — With thy soldiers.

Fouledst — Didst spoil all the conveniences of thy neighbours.

Verse 3

3 Thus saith the Lord GOD; I will therefore spread out my net over thee with a company of many people; and they shall bring thee up in my net.

With a company — In the countries, where these creatures were hunted, they went in mighty companies.

Verse 4

4 Then will I leave thee upon the land, I will cast thee forth upon the open field, and will cause all the fowls of the heaven to remain upon thee, and I will fill the beasts of the whole earth with thee.

Leave thee — This was literally fulfilled in the deserts of Lybia, where the slain of Hophra's army, were left to be devoured by fowls and beasts.

Verse 5

5 And I will lay thy flesh upon the mountains, and fill the valleys with thy height.

With thy height — With the carcasses of thy princes.

Verse 6

6 I will also water with thy blood the land wherein thou swimmest, even to the mountains; and the rivers shall be full of thee.

Even to the mountains — Blood shall be poured forth, as if it were to rise to the very mountains.

Full of thee — O thy blood, and of thy carcasses cast into them.

Verse 7

7 And when I shall put thee out, I will cover the heaven, and make the stars thereof dark; I will cover the sun with a cloud, and the moon shall not give her light.

Put thee out — As a torch is extinguished.

Cover the sun — Probably some unusual darkness was seen in the heavens, and on the earth, about that time.

Verse 9

9 I will also vex the hearts of many people, when I shall bring thy destruction among the nations, into the countries which thou hast not known.

Thy destruction — The fame of it.

Not known — Such as were strangers to Egypt, shall be troubled with apprehension of what mischief may come upon the world from so mighty a conqueror.

Verse 10

10 Yea, I will make many people amazed at thee, and their kings shall be horribly afraid for thee, when I shall brandish my sword before them; and they shall tremble at every moment, every man for his own life, in the day of thy fall.

Shall tremble — Be greatly afraid, lest Nebuchadnezzar, who is God's sword, should smite them.

Every man — Every one of the kings, whose kingdoms are near to Egypt.

Verse 13

13 I will destroy also all the beasts thereof from beside the great waters; neither shall the foot of man trouble them any more, nor the hoofs of beasts trouble them.

All the beasts — The sheep, and oxen devoured, or driven away: the horses taken up to mount the horsemen, whose own horses were tired, or spoiled.

Great waters — The pasture lying along the river side.

Trouble them — There shall be so few men left in Egypt, that they shall not as formerly, disturb the waters by digging, swimming, or rowing on them.

Nor the hoofs — So few horses or cows, that they shall not at watering-times, or in the heat of the day, foul the waters.

Verse 14

14 Then will I make their waters deep, and cause their rivers to run like oil, saith the Lord GOD.

Like oil — A figurative expression, signifying, there shall be such an universal sadness and heaviness upon the whole nation, that the very rivers which used to flow briskly, shall grow deep, and slow, and heavy.

Verse 15

15 When I shall make the land of Egypt desolate, and the country shall be destitute of that whereof it was full, when I shall smite all them that dwell therein, then shall they know that I am the LORD.

Of that — Men and women, cattle, wealth, and peace.

Verse 16

16 This is the lamentation wherewith they shall lament her: the daughters of the nations shall lament her: they shall lament for her, even for Egypt, and for all her multitude, saith the Lord GOD.

This is the lamentation — This mournful account, which the prophet has given of Egypt.

Verse 18

18 Son of man, wail for the multitude of Egypt, and cast them down, even her, and the daughters of the famous nations, unto the nether parts of the earth, with them that go down into the pit.

Wail — Prepare the funeral ceremonies at the burial of Egypt.

The daughters — And celebrate the funerals of other cities and kingdoms that lie buried in their own ruins.

The nether parts of the earth — A well known description of the state of the dead.

The pit — The Egyptians affected to be buried in the Pyramids, and their kings, and great ones, would be laid by themselves; but Ezekiel provides them their grave among common people, being buried just where they fall.

Verse 19

19 Whom dost thou pass in beauty? go down, and be thou laid with the uncircumcised.

Whom — Art thou better than others that thou shouldest not die, and be laid in the dust, as well as they.

Go — Go down like others.

With the uncircumcised — Among profane and loathed carcasses, such the uncircumcised were in the opinion of the circumcised, as were the Egyptians.

Verse 20

20 They shall fall in the midst of them that are slain by the sword: she is delivered to the sword: draw her and all her multitudes.

They — The Egyptians.

She — The whole Egyptian kingdom.

Draw — And throw them together into the pit.

Verse 21

21 The strong among the mighty shall speak to him out of the midst of hell with them that help him: they are gone down, they lie uncircumcised, slain by the sword.

Him — The king of Egypt.

The grave — Where they lie without strength, as dead mortals, tho' while they lived, they bore themselves, as gods.

That help — His helpers, dead before him, shall speak to him.

Gone down — To the grave.

They lie — Neglected, and forgotten.

Verse 22

22 Asshur is there and all her company: his graves are about him: all of them slain, fallen by the sword:

Ashur — The famous, warlike, king of Assyria.

Is there — In the state of the dead, in the land of darkness and oblivion.

Her company — Princes, soldiers, subjects, and confederates.

Are about him — They are about him, who were slain with him.

Verse 23

23 Whose graves are set in the sides of

the pit, and her company is round about her grave: all of them slain, fallen by the sword, which caused terror in the land of the living.

Whose graves — Here is supposed a spacious vault, in the midst whereof the king of Ashur lies, and round the vault, his familiar captains and commanders.

Her company — The common subjects of the Assyrian empire, all buried undistinguished about her.

Her grave — The ruins of an empire are its grave.

In the land — While they were in the land of the living.

Verse 24

24 There is Elam and all her multitude round about her grave, all of them slain, fallen by the sword, which are gone down uncircumcised into the nether parts of the earth, which caused their terror in the land of the living; yet have they borne their shame with them that go down to the pit.

Elam — The Persians, and their famous kings, who lived in former days.

Their shame — God, and man poured contempt upon them, and turned their glory into shame.

Verse 25

25 They have set her a bed in the midst of the slain with all her multitude: her graves are round about him: all of them uncircumcised, slain by the sword: though their terror was caused in the land of the living, yet have they borne their shame with them that go down to the pit: he is put in the midst of them that be slain.

A bed — The Persians had their coffins, in which with balms and spices, the dead were kept, in the midst of places provided for them; in such is the king of Elam here placed with his slaughtered captains about him. All the honour he can now pretend to, is to be buried in the chief sepulchre.

Verse 26

26 There is Meshech, Tubal, and all her multitude: her graves are round about him: all of them uncircumcised, slain by the sword, though they caused their terror in the land of the living.

Her multitude — With the Cappadocians and Albanians, the Scythians may be included, many of whom were next neighbors to them.

Verse 27

27 And they shall not lie with the mighty that are fallen of the uncircumcised, which are gone down to hell with their weapons of war: and they have laid their swords under their heads, but their iniquities shall be upon their bones, though they were the terror of the mighty in the land of the living.

They — The leaders of these Scythians were not buried with a pomp like that of Ashur, or Elan, but surprised by Halyattes and Cyaxares, were cut off with all their multitude, and tumbled into pits with the rabble.

With their weapons — A ceremony observed in pompous funerals of great captains, to have their weapons, and their armour carried before the hearse.

Laid their swords — In their graves, as if they could sleep the sweeter there, when they laid their heads on such a pillow: These barbarous Scythians were not so buried.

Their iniquity — The exemplary punishment of their iniquity shall be seen upon their bones unburied.

Verse 28

28 Yea, thou shalt be broken in the midst of the uncircumcised, and shalt lie with them that are slain with the sword.

Thou — Chief of Mesech, and Tubal.

Shalt be broken — Shalt be killed with the rest of thy wicked followers.

Shalt lie — Without regard, hurled into the pit with common soldiers.

Verse 29

29 There is Edom, her kings, and all her princes, which with their might are laid by them that were slain by the sword: they shall lie with the uncircumcised, and with them that go down to the pit.

With the uncircumcised — The Edomites retained circumcision, being of the seed of Abraham. But that shall stand them in no stead: they shall lie with the uncircumcised.

Verse 30

30 There be the princes of the north, all of them, and all the Zidonians, which are gone down with the slain; with their terror they are ashamed of their might; and they lie uncircumcised with them that be slain by the sword, and bear their shame with them that go down to the pit.

Of the north — Tyrians, Assyrians, and Syrians, who lay northward from Judea, now swallowed up by the Babylonian.

Of their might — When it appeared too weak to resist the enemy.

Uncircumcised — Scorned, and cast out as profane and loathsome.

Verse 31

31 Pharaoh shall see them, and shall be comforted over all his multitude, even Pharaoh and all his army slain by the sword, saith the Lord GOD.

Comforted — Poor comfort! Yet all that he will find!

Verse 32

32 For I have caused my terror in the land of the living: and he shall be laid in the midst of the uncircumcised with them that are slain with the sword, even Pharaoh and all his multitude, saith the Lord GOD.

My terror — These tyrants were a terror to the world by their cruelty; and God hath made them a terror by his just punishments; and so, saith God, will I do with Pharaoh. Come and see the calamitous state of human life! See what a dying world this is! The strong die, the mighty die; Pharaoh and all his multitude! But here is likewise an allusion to the final and everlasting death of impenitent sinners. Those that are uncircumcised in heart, are slain by the sword of Divine Justice. Their iniquity is upon them, and they bear their shame for ever.

Chapter Thirty-Three

The duty of a spiritual watchman, ver. 1 - 9.

A declaration of the safety of penitents,

and the destruction of apostates, ver. 10 - 20.

A message to those who flattered themselves with hopes of safety, tho' they repented not, ver. 21 - 29.

A reproof of those who approved the word of God, but did not practise it, ver. 30 - 33.

Verse 6

6 But if the watchman see the sword come, and blow not the trumpet, and the people be not warned; if the sword come, and take any person from among them, he is taken away in his iniquity; but his blood will I require at the watchman's hand.

Is taken away — Punished by the Lord for his sin.

Verse 10

10 Therefore, O thou son of man, speak unto the house of Israel; Thus ye speak, saying, If our transgressions and our sins be upon us, and we pine away in them, how should we then live?

Our sins — The unpardoned guilt, and the unsupportable punishment of our sins, in the wasting of our country, burning our city, abolishing the publick worship of God; we shall pine away, 'tis too late to hope.

How — How can it be better with us?

Verse 21

21 And it came to pass in the twelfth year of our captivity, in the tenth month, in the fifth day of the month, that one that had escaped out of Jerusalem came unto me, saying, The city is smitten.

Smitten — Taken and plundered.

Verse 22

22 Now the hand of the LORD was upon me in the evening, afore he that was escaped came; and had opened my mouth, until he came to me in the morning; and my mouth was opened, and I was no more dumb.

Opened my mouth — Not that the prophet was utterly dumb before, for he had prophesied against many nations, only he was forbidden to say anything of the Jews, But now the spirit moved him to speak, and continued his motion, 'till the messenger came, and ever after.

Verse 24

24 Son of man, they that inhabit those wastes of the land of Israel speak, saying, Abraham was one, and he inherited the land: but we are many; the land is given us for inheritance.

They — Who were left behind, now come out of their holes, or returned from neighbouring countries, or permitted by the conqueror to stay and plant vineyards.

Wastes — Places once fruitful and abounding with people, but now, made a desolate wilderness.

He inherited — Our father had a right to all this land, when but one; we his children though diminished, are many, and the divine goodness will surely continue to us both right and possession.

Is given — It was given by promise to us, the seed, as well as to our progenitor; nay more, 'tis given us in possession, whereas Abraham had not one foot of it.

Verse 26

26 Ye stand upon your sword, ye work abomination, and ye defile every one his neighbour's wife: and shall ye possess the land?

Ye stand — You trust to your sword; you do all with violence.

Abominations — Idolatry.

Verse 30

30 Also, thou son of man, the children of thy people still are talking against thee by the walls and in the doors of the houses, and speak one to another, every one to his brother, saying, Come, I pray you, and hear what is the word that cometh forth from the LORD.

The children — Captives in Babylon.

Verse 31

31 And they come unto thee as the people cometh, and they sit before thee as my people, and they hear thy words, but they will not do them: for with their mouth they shew much love, but their heart goeth after their covetousness.

They come — As if they were really the people of God.

They sit — So we find the elders of Judah, chap. 8:1, so the disciples of the rabbis sat at their feet.

Chapter Thirty-Four

A charge against the shepherds of Israel, ver. 1 - 6.
Their dismission from their trust, ver. 7 - 10.
A promise, that God would take care of his flock, ver. 11 - 16.
Another charge against the strong of the flock, for their injuring the weak, ver. 17 - 22.
A promise of the Messiah, the great and good shepherd, ver. 23 - 31.

Verse 2

2 Son of man, prophesy against the shepherds of Israel, prophesy, and say unto them, Thus saith the Lord GOD unto the shepherds; Woe be to the shepherds of Israel that do feed themselves! should not the shepherds feed the flocks?

The shepherds — The rulers of the people kings, magistrates, and princes; as also priests, and prophets.

Of Israel — The two tribes, and the few out of the ten that adhere to the house of David.

That feed — Contrive their own ease, advantage, and honour.

Verse 3

3 Ye eat the fat, and ye clothe you with the wool, ye kill them that are fed: but ye feed not the flock.

Ye kill — You contrive methods, to take first the life, and next the estate of the well-fed, the rich and wealthy.

But — You take care to lead, protect, provide for, and watch over them.

Verse 4

4 The diseased have ye not strengthened, neither have ye healed that which was sick, neither have ye bound up that which was broken, neither have ye brought again that which was driven away, neither have ye sought that which was lost; but with force and with cruelty have ye ruled them.

The diseased — The weak and languishing.

Bound up — Oppressors in the state, or church, broke many then, but these shepherds bound them not up.

Verse 5

5 And they were scattered, because there is no shepherd: and they became meat to all the beasts of the field, when they were scattered.

No shepherd — No vigilant, faithful shepherd.

Became meat — Were made a prey of, and devoured by all their neighbours.

Verse 12

12 As a shepherd seeketh out his flock in the day that he is among his sheep that are scattered; so will I seek out my sheep, and will deliver them out of all places where they have been scattered in the cloudy and dark day.

In the cloudy and dark day — In the time of general distress.

Verse 16

16 I will seek that which was lost, and bring again that which was driven away, and will bind up that which was broken, and will strengthen that which was sick: but I will destroy the fat and the strong; I will feed them with judgment.

The fat — The powerful and rich.

I will feed — I will judge and punish them.

Verse 17

17 And as for you, O my flock, thus saith the Lord GOD; Behold, I judge between cattle and cattle, between the rams and the he goats.

I judge — Between men and men, between the smaller and weaker, and the greater and stronger, as their different state requires I will do.

The rams — Rulers, who also shalt be dealt with according to their behaviour.

Verse 18

18 Seemeth it a small thing unto you to have eaten up the good pasture, but ye must tread down with your feet the residue of your pastures? and to have drunk of the deep waters, but ye must foul the residue with your feet?

But ye must tread down — You great ones, eat the fat, and sweet; and what you cannot eat, you waste and spoil.

The deep waters — Which are sufficient for all.

Verse 20

20 Therefore thus saith the Lord GOD unto them; Behold, I, even I, will judge between the fat cattle and between the lean cattle.

I will judge — I will vindicate the poor.

The fat cattle — The rich.

The lean — The poor.

Verse 23

23 And I will set up one shepherd over them, and he shall feed them, even my servant David; he shall feed them, and he shall be their shepherd.

One shepherd — Christ, the great

good, chief, only shepherd, that laid down his life for his sheep.

My servant David — The seed of David, the beloved one, who was typified by David, and is in other places called by his name, as Jeremiah 30:9; Ezekiel 37:24; Hosea 3:5.

He shall feed — Do all the office of a good and faithful shepherd, and that for ever.

Verse 24

24 And I the LORD will be their God, and my servant David a prince among them; I the LORD have spoken it.

My servant — Christ was in this great work his fathers servant, Isaiah 42:1.

Verse 25

25 And I will make with them a covenant of peace, and will cause the evil beasts to cease out of the land: and they shall dwell safely in the wilderness, and sleep in the woods.

A covenant — A covenant of promises, which contain, and shall bring peace, that is all good.

Verse 26

26 And I will make them and the places round about my hill a blessing; and I will cause the shower to come down in his season; there shall be showers of blessing.

Them — My returned captives, The places - All the country.

My hill — Jerusalem.

Verse 29

29 And I will raise up for them a plant of renown, and they shall be no more consumed with hunger in the land, neither bear the shame of the heathen any more.

A plant — The Messiah.

The shame — The reproach.

Verse 30

30 Thus shall they know that I the LORD their God am with them, and that they, even the house of Israel, are my people, saith the Lord GOD.

Their God — By covenant, from their forefathers.

Am with them — Present with them, and reconciled to them.

Chapter Thirty-Five

A prophecy against Edom for their hatred to Israel, ver. 1 - 13.
Their ruin shall be perpetual, ver. 14, 15.

Verse 2

2 Son of man, set thy face against mount Seir, and prophesy against it,

Mount Seir — The Edomites, who inhabited it.

Verse 5

5 Because thou hast had a perpetual hatred, and hast shed the blood of the children of Israel by the force of the sword in the time of their calamity, in the time that their iniquity had an end:

Their iniquity — When their iniquity was punished on them, which brought them to final ruin.

Verse 6

6 Therefore, as I live, saith the Lord GOD, I will prepare thee unto blood, and blood shall pursue thee: sith thou hast not hated blood, even blood shall pursue thee.

And blood — Thy guilt, and my just revenge of innocent blood.

Hast not hated — Thou hast loved, rather than hated, blood-shed; therefore vengeance for it follows thee.

Verse 7

7 Thus will I make mount Seir most desolate, and cut off from it him that passeth out and him that returneth.

That passeth out — All travellers that go to or from Edom.

Verse 9

9 I will make thee perpetual desolations, and thy cities shall not return: and ye shall know that I am the LORD.

Return — To their former glory.

Verse 10

10 Because thou hast said, These two nations and these two countries shall be mine, and we will possess it; whereas the LORD was there:

Though — Though God was with Israel.

Verse 11

11 Therefore, as I live, saith the Lord GOD, I will even do according to thine anger, and according to thine envy which thou hast used out of thy hatred against them; and I will make myself known among them, when I have judged thee.

Judged — Punished thee.

Verse 14

14 Thus saith the Lord GOD; When the whole earth rejoiceth, I will make thee desolate.

The whole earth — The inhabitants of all the countries round about thee.

Rejoiceth — Is in peace and plenty.

Chapter Thirty-Six

A promise of the restoration of Israel, from their present deplorable condition, ver. 1 - 15.
They are reminded of their former sins, and God's judgments, ver. 16 - 20.
A promise of pardon, ver, 21 - 24.
And sanctification, 25 - 38.

Verse 1

1 Also, thou son of man, prophesy unto the mountains of Israel, and say, Ye mountains of Israel, hear the word of the LORD:

The mountains — The inhabitants being in captivity, speak to the mountains, that is, the land of Judah, and Israel, which was a country full of mountains.

Verse 2

2 Thus saith the Lord GOD; Because the enemy hath said against you, Aha, even the ancient high places are ours in possession:

Because the enemy — Many were the enemies of God's people; but they so conspired in one design, that the prophet speaks of them as one, and particularly of Edom.

Verse 3

3 Therefore prophesy and say, Thus saith the Lord GOD; Because they have made you desolate, and swallowed you up on every side, that ye might be a possession unto the residue of the heathen, and ye are taken up in the lips of talkers, and are an infamy of the people:

Swallowed — Devoured you, as hungry beasts devour their prey.

Ye are taken up — You are the subject of all their discourse.

An infamy — Ever branding you as infamous.

Verse 7

7 Therefore thus saith the Lord GOD; I have lifted up mine hand, Surely the heathen that are about you, they shall bear their shame.

Lifted up mine hand — Sworn in my wrath.

The heathen — The Moabites, Ammonites, and Idumeans.

Verse 8

8 But ye, O mountains of Israel, ye shall shoot forth your branches, and yield your fruit to my people of Israel; for they are at hand to come.

At hand — The time is near, when my people shall come out of Babylon to settle in their own land.

Verse 12

12 Yea, I will cause men to walk upon you, even my people Israel; and they shall possess thee, and thou shalt be their inheritance, and thou shalt no more henceforth bereave them of men.

And thou — O land of Canaan.

Bereave — Consume thine inhabitants.

Verse 13

13 Thus saith the Lord GOD; Because they say unto you, Thou land devourest up men, and hast bereaved thy nations;

They — The heathen round about.

Verse 14

14 Therefore thou shalt devour men no more, neither bereave thy nations any more, saith the Lord GOD.

Therefore — I will so bless thee, O land, that thou shalt bring forth and breed up many sons and daughters, and this reproach shall cease for ever.

Verse 17

17 Son of man, when the house of Israel dwelt in their own land, they defiled it by their own way and by their doings: their way was before me as the uncleanness of a removed woman.

By their doings — By their carriage, and whole conversation.

As the uncleanness — Or as one cut off from the congregation, because of some great sin.

Verse 20

20 And when they entered unto the heathen, whither they went, they profaned my holy name, when they said to them, These are the people of the LORD, and are gone forth out of his land.

Entered — When they were come into Babylon.

Profaned — They sinned.

They — Their heathen neighbours.

Them — The profane Jews.

These — These profane slaves, call themselves the people of the Lord and say, he gave them the land out of which they are driven.

Verse 21

21 But I had pity for mine holy name, which the house of Israel had profaned among the heathen, whither they went.

But I had pity — For these sins I had just cause to cut them off; but I had pity, for the glory of my name: had I destroyed them, the heathen would have concluded against my omnipotence, and my truth.

Verse 23

23 And I will sanctify my great name, which was profaned among the heathen, which ye have profaned in the midst of them; and the heathen shall know that I am the LORD, saith the Lord GOD, when I shall be sanctified in you before their eyes.

I will sanctify my great name — They gave the heathen occasion to think meanly of me, but I will shew I am as great as good. When God performs what he hath sworn by his holiness, then he sanctifies his name.

Verse 25

25 Then will I sprinkle clean water upon you, and ye shall be clean: from all your filthiness, and from all your idols, will I cleanse you.

Sprinkle — "This signifies both the blood of Christ sprinkled upon their conscience, to take away their guilt, as the water of purification was sprinkled, to take away their ceremonial uncleanness and the grace of the spirit sprinkled on the whole soul, to purify it from all corrupt inclinations and dispositions."

Verse 26

26 A new heart also will I give you, and a new spirit will I put within you: and I will take away the stony heart out of your flesh, and I will give you an heart of flesh.

A new heart — A new frame of soul, a mind changed, from sinful to holy, from carnal to spiritual. A heart in which the law of God is written, Jeremiah 31:33. A sanctified heart, in which the almighty grace of God is victorious, and turns it from all sin to God.

A new spirit — A new, holy frame in the spirit of man; which is given to him, not wrought by his own power.

The stony — The senseless unfeeling.

Out of your flesh — Out of you.

Of flesh — That is, quite of another temper, hearkening to God's law, trembling at his threats, moulded into a compliance with his whole will; to forbear, do, be, or suffer what God will, receiving the impress of God, as soft wax receives the impress of the seal.

Verse 27

27 And I will put my spirit within you, and cause you to walk in my statutes, and ye shall keep my judgments, and do them.

My spirit — The holy spirit of God, which is given to, and dwelleth in all true believers.

And cause you — Sweetly, powerfully, yet without compulsion; for our spirits, framed by God's spirit to a disposition suitable to his holiness, readily concurs.

Ye shall keep — Be willing; and able to keep the judgments, and to walk in the statutes of God, which is, to live in all holiness.

Verse 28

28 And ye shall dwell in the land that I gave to your fathers; and ye shall be my people, and I will be your God.

Ye shall dwell — Observe: then, and not before, are these promises to be fulfilled to the house of Israel.

And I will be your God — This is the foundation of the top-stone of a believer's happiness.

Verse 29

29 I will also save you from all your uncleannesses: and I will call for the corn, and will increase it, and lay no famine upon you.

I will also save you — I will continue to save you.

From all your uncleannesses — Salvation from all uncleannessess, includes justification, entire sanctification, and meetness for glory.

The corn — All necessaries comprised in one.

Verse 35

35 And they shall say, This land that was desolate is become like the garden of Eden; and the waste and desolate and ruined cities are become fenced, and are inhabited.

And they — Strangers, or foreigners.

Verse 37

37 Thus saith the Lord GOD; I will yet for this be enquired of by the house of Israel, to do it for them; I will increase them with men like a flock.

Enquired of — Though I have repeated so often my promise to do this, yet it is their duty to intreat it, to wait on me, and then I will do it.

Verse 38

38 As the holy flock, as the flock of Jerusalem in her solemn feasts; so shall the waste cities be filled with flocks of men: and they shall know that I am the LORD.

As the holy flock — Flocks designed to holy uses.

In her solemn feasts — These flocks were for quality, the best of all; and for numbers, very great, on the solemn feasts. Thus shall men multiply, and fill the cities of replanted Judea. And the increase of the numbers of men is then honourable, when they are all dedicated to God as a holy flock, to be presented to him for living sacrifices. Crowds are a lovely sight in God's temple.

Chapter Thirty-Seven

The vision of the resurrection of the dry bones, ver. 1 - 10.
The explication of it, ver. 11 - 14.
A type of the happy coalition which would be between Israel and Judah, ver. 15 - 22.

A prediction of the kingdom of Christ, and of the glories and graces of that kingdom, ver. 23 - 28.

Verse 1

1 The hand of the LORD was upon me, and carried me out in the spirit of the LORD, and set me down in the midst of the valley which was full of bones,

And set me down — So it seemed to me in the vision. Which is a lively representation of a threefold resurrection: 1. Of the resurrection of souls, from the death of sin, to the life of righteousness: 2. The resurrection of the church from an afflicted state, to liberty and peace: 3. The resurrection of the body at the great day, especially the bodies of believers to life eternal.

Verse 3

3 And he said unto me, Son of man, can these bones live? And I answered, O Lord GOD, thou knowest.

And he — The Lord.

Verse 7

7 So I prophesied as I was commanded: and as I prophesied, there was a noise, and behold a shaking, and the bones came together, bone to his bone.

Prophesied — Declared these promises.

As I prophesied — While I was prophesying.

A noise — A rattling of the bones in their motion.

A shaking — A trembling or commotion among the bones, enough to manifest a divine presence, working among them.

Came together — Glided nearer and nearer, 'till each bone met the bone to which it was to be joined. Of all the bones of all those numerous slain, not one was missing, not one missed its way, not one missed its place, but each knew and found its fellow. Thus in the resurrection of the dead, the scattered atoms shall be arranged in their proper place and order, and every bone come to his bone, by the same wisdom and power by which they were first formed in the womb of her that is with child.

Verse 8

8 And when I beheld, lo, the sinews and the flesh came up upon them, and the skin covered them above: but there was no breath in them.

Came up — Gradually spreading itself.

Verse 9

9 Then said he unto me, Prophesy unto the wind, prophesy, son of man, and say to the wind, Thus saith the Lord GOD; Come from the four winds, O breath, and breathe upon these slain, that they may live.

Prophesy — Declare what my will is.

O breath — The soul, whose emblem here is wind; which, as it gently blew upon these lifeless creatures, each was inspired with its own soul or spirit.

Verse 10

10 So I prophesied as he commanded me, and the breath came into them, and they lived, and stood up upon their feet, an exceeding great army.

And the breath — The spirit of life, or the soul, Genesis 2:7.

Verse 11

11 Then he said unto me, Son of man, these bones are the whole house of Israel: behold, they say, Our bones are dried, and our hope is lost: we are cut off for our parts.

The whole house — The emblem of the house of Israel.

Are dried — Our state is as hopeless, as far from recovery, as dried bones are from life.

Verse 12

12 Therefore prophesy and say unto them, Thus saith the Lord GOD; Behold, O my people, I will open your graves, and cause you to come up out of your graves, and bring you into the land of Israel.

I will open — Though your captivity be as death, your persons close as the grave, yet I will open those graves.

Verse 16

16 Moreover, thou son of man, take thee one stick, and write upon it, For Judah, and for the children of Israel his companions: then take another stick, and write upon it, For Joseph, the stick of Ephraim, and for all the house of Israel his companions:

One stick — A writing tablet or a tally, such as is fit to be written upon.

His companions — Benjamin and part of Levi, who kept with the tribe of Judah.

Ephraim — Ephraim was the most considerable tribe in the kingdom of Israel, when divided from the other two.

The house of Israel — The other nine tribes, who continued with Ephraim.

Verse 19

19 Say unto them, Thus saith the Lord GOD; Behold, I will take the stick of Joseph, which is in the hand of Ephraim, and the tribes of Israel his fellows, and will put them with him, even with the stick of Judah, and make them one stick, and they shall be one in mine hand.

In mine hand — Under my government, care, and blessing. God will make the two kingdoms one in his hand, as I make these two sticks one in my hand.

Verse 22

22 And I will make them one nation in the land upon the mountains of Israel; and one king shall be king to them all: and they shall be no more two nations, neither shall they be divided into two kingdoms any more at all:

One nation — They were one in David's time, who was a type of the Messiah, and continued so to the end of Solomon's time, whose name includes peace. So when the Beloved, the Peace-maker, the Messiah shall be king, they shall be one again.

And one king — The Messiah.

Verse 23

23 Neither shall they defile themselves any more with their idols, nor with their detestable things, nor with any of their transgressions: but I will save them out of all their dwellingplaces, wherein they have sinned, and will cleanse them: so shall they be my people, and I will be their God.

I will save — I will bring them safe out of them.

And will cleanse — Both justify and sanctify them.

Verse 24

24 And David my servant shall be king over them; and they all shall have one shepherd: they shall also walk in my judgments, and observe my statutes, and do them.

David — The son of David.

One shepherd — This king shall be their one chief shepherd, others that feed and rule the flock, are so by commission from him.

Verse 25

25 And they shall dwell in the land that I have given unto Jacob my servant, wherein your fathers have dwelt; and they shall dwell therein, even they, and their children, and their children's children for ever: and my servant David shall be their prince for ever.

For ever — 'Till Christ's coming to judgment, the Jews converted to Christ, shall inherit Canaan.

Verse 26

26 Moreover I will make a covenant of peace with them; it shall be an everlasting covenant with them: and I will place them, and multiply them, and will set my sanctuary in the midst of them for evermore.

My sanctuary — I will set up a spiritual glorious temple, and worship among you.

For evermore — Never to be altered or abolished on earth, but to be consummated in heaven.

Verse 27

27 My tabernacle also shall be with them: yea, I will be their God, and they shall be my people.

My tabernacle — The tabernacle wherein I will shew my presence among them. Their fathers had a tabernacle, but the Messiah shall bring with him a better, a spiritual, and an heavenly.

They shall be my people — By my grace I will make them holy, as the people of a holy God; and I will make them happy, as the people of the ever blessed God.

Chapter Thirty-Eight

The attempt of Gog and Magog on the land of Israel, ver. 1 - 13.
The terror occasioned thereby, ver. 14 - 20.
Their defeat by the immediate hand of God, ver. 21 - 23.

Verse 1

1 And the word of the LORD came unto me, saying,

Saying — God now forewarns the Jews, what enemies and troubles would interpose, before he would fully deliver them.

Verse 2

2 Son of man, set thy face against Gog, the land of Magog, the chief prince of Meshech and Tubal, and prophesy against him,

Gog — This cannot be one single person, or prince, though perhaps it points out some one, by whom the troubles foretold were begun. Some believe the time is still to come, wherein this prophecy is to be fulfilled. And that it must intend those enemies of God's church who descended from the Scythians, and are now masters of Cappadocia, Iberia, Armenia, or are in confederacy with the Tartars, and those northern heathens. But others think, all the enemies of Israel in all quarters, both open and secret are here intended, and that the Antichristian forces and combination, are what the prophet foretells.

Magog — Magog is, at least, part of Scythia, and comprehends Syria, in which was Hierapolis. taken by the Scythians, and called of them Scythopolis. It is that country, which now is in subjection to the Turks, and may be extended thro' Asia minor, the countries of Sarmatia, and many others, under more than one in succession of time. And in the last time under some one active and daring prince, all their power will be stirred up against Christians.

Verse 4

4 And I will turn thee back, and put hooks into thy jaws, and I will bring thee forth, and all thine army, horses and horsemen, all of them clothed with all sorts of armour, even a great company with bucklers and shields, all of them handling swords:

Handling swords — That is, very ready, expert and strong in using the sword.

Verse 6

6 Gomer, and all his bands; the house of Togarmah of the north quarters, and all his bands: and many people with thee.

Gomer — Inhabitants of Galatia.

Togarmah — Paphlagonia, and Cappadocia.

The north quarters — The more northern people, the numerous Tartars.

Verse 7

7 Be thou prepared, and prepare for thyself, thou, and all thy company that are assembled unto thee, and be thou a guard unto them.

Be thou prepared — God and the church deride this mighty preparation.

Verse 8

8 After many days thou shalt be visited: in the latter years thou shalt come into the land that is brought back from the sword, and is gathered out of many people, against the mountains of Israel, which have been always waste: but it is brought forth out of the nations, and they shall dwell safely all of them.

After many days — In the latter days of the Messiah's kingdom among men.

In the later years — These must be cotemporary with the many days already mentioned.

Thou — Gog with all thy numbers.

The land — The land of the Jews, a people recovered from captivity, into which the sword of their enemy had brought them.

Always waste — It is already two thousand four hundred years since the ten tribes were carried away by Salmanezer.

But it — The land of Canaan, that is,

112

the people of it.

Verse 11

11 And thou shalt say, I will go up to the land of unwalled villages; I will go to them that are at rest, that dwell safely, all of them dwelling without walls, and having neither bars nor gates,

Unwalled — Weak, and without any considerable defences.

Verse 13

13 Sheba, and Dedan, and the merchants of Tarshish, with all the young lions thereof, shall say unto thee, Art thou come to take a spoil? hast thou gathered thy company to take a prey? to carry away silver and gold, to take away cattle and goods, to take a great spoil?

Sheba — This Sheba was southward, and contains all of that coast which assisted Gog.

Dedan — By these are noted, the eastern nations that assisted.

Tarshish — The inhabitants of the sea-coast westward, and Magog north.

The young lions — Young men thirsty of blood, but more of spoil, resolve to join, if they may rob and spoil for themselves.

Art thou come — This repeated enquiry seems to be an agreement to come to his assistance, on condition they might have, possess, and carry away what they seize.

Verse 14

14 Therefore, son of man, prophesy and say unto Gog, Thus saith the Lord GOD; In that day when my people of Israel dwelleth safely, shalt thou not know it?

Know it — Thou wilt be informed of it.

Verse 15

15 And thou shalt come from thy place out of the north parts, thou, and many people with thee, all of them riding upon horses, a great company, and a mighty army:

The north parts — From Scythia, from the Euxine and Caspian seas, and countries thereabouts.

Verse 16

16 And thou shalt come up against my people of Israel, as a cloud to cover the land; it shall be in the latter days, and I will bring thee against my land, that the heathen may know me, when I shall be sanctified in thee, O Gog, before their eyes.

I will bring — I will permit thee to come.

Sanctified — Confessed to be a great God over all, a gracious and faithful God to his people, and a dreadful enemy and avenger against the wicked.

Before — In the sight of all the heathen that are with Gog, and much more in the sight of God's own people.

Verse 17

17 Thus saith the Lord GOD; Art thou he of whom I have spoken in old time by my servants the prophets of Israel, which prophesied in those days many years that I would bring thee against them?

Spoken — All these enterprises I have

spoken of, and will as well defeat as I did foretel them.

Verse 19

19 For in my jealousy and in the fire of my wrath have I spoken, Surely in that day there shall be a great shaking in the land of Israel;

For — For my own people, and for mine own glory.

Have I spoken — Against mine enemies Gog, and all his herd.

A great shaking — A great disturbance and tumult, like an earthquake.

Verse 21

21 And I will call for a sword against him throughout all my mountains, saith the Lord GOD: every man's sword shall be against his brother.

Sword — Israel.

Throughout — From all parts of the land, which was full of mountains.

Every man's sword — As it was in Jehoshaphat's time; and these swords may be meant by the sword God will call for through all, for they ranged all over his mountains.

Verse 23

23 Thus will I magnify myself, and sanctify myself; and I will be known in the eyes of many nations, and they shall know that I am the LORD.

Magnify — Undeniably prove that I am the mighty, just, faithful, wise, holy, and merciful God.

Sanctify — Declare I am holy, and true to my word.

Chapter Thirty-Nine

A prediction of the utter destruction of Gog and Magog, ver. 1 - 7.
An illustration of the vastness of that destruction, ver. 8 - 22.
God's mercy to his people, ver. 23 - 29.

Verse 2

2 And I will turn thee back, and leave but the sixth part of thee, and will cause thee to come up from the north parts, and will bring thee upon the mountains of Israel:

The sixth part — I will leave in thy country but one in six.

Verse 3

3 And I will smite thy bow out of thy left hand, and will cause thine arrows to fall out of thy right hand.

Thy bow — What is said of the bow rendered useless, is to be understood of all other weapons of war; this is one kind, the bow, being most in use with the Scythians, is mentioned for all the rest.

Verse 8

8 Behold, it is come, and it is done, saith the Lord GOD; this is the day whereof I have spoken.

It is come — As sure as if already come.

The day — That notable day of recompences against the last great enemies of the church.

Verse 9

9 And they that dwell in the cities of Israel shall go forth, and shall set on fire and burn the weapons, both the shields and the bucklers, the bows and the arrows, and the handstaves, and the spears, and they shall burn them with fire seven years:

The weapons — The warlike provision, instruments, engines, carriages and wagons.

Shall burn — It may be wondered why they burn these weapons, which might be of use to them for defence; but it was done in testimony that God was their defence, on whom only they relied.

With fire — In such a country where the need of fire is much less than with us, it will not seem incredible, that the warlike utensils of so numerous an army might be enough to furnish them with fuel for many years.

Verse 11

11 And it shall come to pass in that day, that I will give unto Gog a place there of graves in Israel, the valley of the passengers on the east of the sea: and it shall stop the noses of the passengers: and there shall they bury Gog and all his multitude: and they shall call it The valley of Hamongog.

Gog — And to many of those with him; but many were given to the birds and beasts to be devoured.

Graves — Gog came to take possession; and so he shall, but not as he purposed and hoped. He shall possess his house of darkness in that land which he invaded.

The valley of the passengers — So called from the frequent travels of passengers through it from Egypt and Arabia Felix, into the more northern parts, and from these again into Egypt and Arabia.

The sea — The Dead Sea.

Hamon Gog — That is, the multitude of Gog.

Verse 13

13 Yea, all the people of the land shall bury them; and it shall be to them a renown the day that I shall be glorified, saith the Lord GOD.

Glorified — The day of my being glorified shall be a renown to Israel.

Verse 14

14 And they shall sever out men of continual employment, passing through the land to bury with the passengers those that remain upon the face of the earth, to cleanse it: after the end of seven months shall they search.

They — The rulers of Israel.

Sever — Chuse out men who shall make it their work.

Passing — To go up and down over the whole land; for many of Gog's wounded, flying soldiers, died in thickets, and corners into which they crept.

The passengers — Whose assistance they would desire of courtesy.

Remain — Unburied by the public labour of the house of Israel during the seven months.

Verse 16

16 And also the name of the city shall be Hamonah. Thus shall they cleanse the land.

The city — That is, the multitude: the city which is next to this common tomb of Gog.

Verse 17

17 And, thou son of man, thus saith the Lord GOD; Speak unto every feathered fowl, and to every beast of the field, Assemble yourselves, and come; gather yourselves on every side to my sacrifice that I do sacrifice for you, even a great sacrifice upon the mountains of Israel, that ye may eat flesh, and drink blood.

I do sacrifice — The punishment of these God calls a sacrifice, which he offers to his own justice.

Upon the mountains — Where more thousands are offered at once, than ever were at any time offered; 'tis a sacrifice so great, that none ever was, or will be like it.

Verse 18

18 Ye shall eat the flesh of the mighty, and drink the blood of the princes of the earth, of rams, of lambs, and of goats, of bullocks, all of them fatlings of Bashan.

Ye shall eat — In these two and the following verses, God takes on him the person of one that makes a feast, invites his guests, and promises to satisfy them. Of the two former, the first is an Enigmatical invitation, or an invitation in a riddle; the latter is the key to this character.

The mighty — Who had great authority, great courage and strength, the giant-like ones, commanders of great note in the army.

Princes — Many princes came with their country men and subjects to assist in this war.

Rams — These are compared to rams which lead the flock.

Lambs — Lambs are the more ordinary in the army.

Goats — Goats signify the more lascivious, and impetuous among them.

Bullocks — Bullocks, such as though more slow, were of great strength.

Fatlings — Well fed.

Bashan — A mountain of most rich, and sweet soil.

Verse 20

20 Thus ye shall be filled at my table with horses and chariots, with mighty men, and with all men of war, saith the Lord GOD.

At my table — In the field where Gog, his princes, and army, are slain, compared to a table.

Horses — Horsemen, not common foot soldiers.

Chariots — The men that ride in them.

Verse 21

21 And I will set my glory among the heathen, and all the heathen shall see my judgment that I have executed, and my hand that I have laid upon them.

All the heathen — In the countries to which the news shall come.

Verse 26

26 After that they have borne their shame, and all their trespasses whereby they have trespassed against me, when they dwelt safely in their land, and none made them afraid.

Their shame — Reproach for their sins.

Chapter Forty

In this and the following chapter, under the type of a temple and altar, priests and sacrifices, is fore shewed, the spiritual worship which should be performed in Gospel times, and that perfected at last in the kingdom of glory: yea probably, in an happy and glorious state of the church on this side heaven:

In this chapter we have,
A general account of the temple and city, ver. 1 - 4.
A particular account of the east-gate, north-gate and south-gate, ver. 5 - 31.
Of the inner court, ver. 32 - 38.
Of the tables, ver. 39 - 43.
Of the lodgings for the singers and the priests, ver. 44 - 47.
Of the porch, ver. 48, 49.

Verse 1

1 In the five and twentieth year of our captivity, in the beginning of the year, in the tenth day of the month, in the fourteenth year after that the city was smitten, in the selfsame day the hand of the LORD was upon me, and brought me thither.

Of our captivity — Of those that were carried away into captivity with Jeconiah eleven years before Jerusalem was burnt. And this falls in with the three thousand three hundred and seventy fourth year of the world, about five hundred and seventy four years before Christ's incarnation.

The beginning — In the month Nisan.

The tenth day — The day that the paschal lamb was to be taken up in order to the feast on the tenth day.

Brought me — To Jerusalem, the place where it did stand.

Verse 2

2 In the visions of God brought he me into the land of Israel, and set me upon a very high mountain, by which was as the frame of a city on the south.

In the visions of God — By this it appears it was not a corporeal transportation of the prophet.

The frame — The portrait of a city.

On the south — On the south of the mountain, where the prophet was set.

Verse 3

3 And he brought me thither, and, behold, there was a man, whose appearance was like the appearance of brass, with a line of flax in his hand, and a measuring reed; and he stood in the gate.

A man — The same no doubt that appeared to the prophet, chap. 1:26, whose name is the branch, and who builds the temple, Zechariah 6:12,13, whose colour was like burnished brass; Revelation 1:15, which speaks glory and strength.

A line — A plumb-line, a mason's line to discover the rectitude of the building, or its defects.

In the gate — In the north gate, next toward the east.

Verse 5

5 And behold a wall on the outside of the house round about, and in the man's hand a measuring reed of six cubits long by the cubit and an hand breadth: so he measured the breadth of the building, one reed; and the height, one reed.

A wall — This was that outmost wall, that compassed the whole mount Sion, upon whose top the temple stood.

The man's hand — Christ, hath, and keeps the reed in his own hand, as the only fit person to take the measures of all.

A measuring reed — Or cane, for this measuring rod was of those canes growing in that country, long, and light, which architects made use of.

Six cubits long — Each cubit consisting of eighteen inches in our common account.

An hand breadth — Added to each six cubits.

The breadth — The thickness of the walls, which were one reed, and one hand's breadth, or three yards, and three inches thick.

Height — And the height equal, taking the measure from the floor on the inside of the wall.

Verse 6

6 Then came he unto the gate which looketh toward the east, and went up the stairs thereof, and measured the threshold of the gate, which was one reed broad; and the other threshold of the gate, which was one reed broad.

The east — Either of one of the inner walls, or of the temple itself.

Went up — 'Till he was got up, he could not measure the threshold, which was at the top of the stairs, and these were ten, if the measurer be supposed in the gate of the house; or eight, if in the gate of the court of the priests; or seven, if in the court of Israel; and each stair was half a cubit in height, too high for him to take the measure of the threshold, if he did not go up the stairs.

The threshold — It is probable he measured the lower threshold first, as next at hand.

The other threshold — The upper threshold, or lintel of the gate, which was of equal dimensions with the lower, three yards and three inches broad, or thick.

Verse 7

7 And every little chamber was one reed long, and one reed broad; and between the little chambers were five cubits; and the threshold of the gate by the porch of the gate within was one reed.

Chamber — Along the wall of the porch were chambers, three on one side, and three on the other, each one reed square.

Five cubits — A space of two yards and one half between each chamber, either filled with some neat posts or pillars, or it may be quite void.

Within — The inward and outward threshold, were of the same measures, and curiously arched over head from side to side, and end to end, which was from east to west.

Verse 8

8 He measured also the porch of the gate within, one reed.

The porch — The posts which were joined together at the top by an arch, and so made the portico.

Verse 9

9 Then measured he the porch of the gate, eight cubits; and the posts thereof, two cubits; and the porch of the gate was inward.

The porch — Probably another porch, or another gate distinct from that, verse 6.

The posts — These were half columns, that from the floor to the height of the wall jetted out, as if one half of the column were in the wall, and the other without, and the protuberance of this half column, was one cubit.

Verse 10

10 And the little chambers of the gate eastward were three on this side, and three on that side; they three were of one measure: and the posts had one measure on this side and on that side.

Chambers — These chambers were for the priests and Levites to lodge in during their ministration.

Verse 11

11 And he measured the breadth of the entry of the gate, ten cubits; and the length of the gate, thirteen cubits.

Of the entry — It is meant of the whole length of the entry, or walk through the porch, to which they ascended by stairs of a semicircular form.

Verse 12

12 The space also before the little chambers was one cubit on this side, and the space was one cubit on that side: and the little chambers were six cubits on this side, and six cubits on that side.

The space — The rails, which were set up at a cubit distance from the front of these little chambers, on the outside for convenient placing of benches for the priests to sit on.

The space — Between the rails, and the chambers.

Verse 13

13 He measured then the gate from the roof of one little chamber to the roof of another: the breadth was five and twenty cubits, door against door.

From the roof — From the extremity of one little chamber on the north side of the gate, to the extremity of the opposite chamber on the south side, and so one cubit and half for the back wall of one chamber, and as much for the back wall of the other chamber, with the length of the chambers, six cubits each, and ten for the breadth of the gate, amounts to twenty five cubits.

Door against door — It seems the doors of the chambers were two in each chamber in the east and west parts, and so exactly set, that the doors being all open you had a clear prospect through all the chambers to the temple.

Verse 14

14 He made also posts of threescore cubits, even unto the post of the court round about the gate.

He made — Measured, and thereby shewed what kind of posts they should be.

Threescore cubits — Probably this refers to the height of this gate built up two stories above the arch, and the posts in their height are only mentioned, but imply all the rest of the building over the east gate.

Unto the post — These high columns, on the inner front of this gate were so disposed, that the last on each side was very near the first post, or pillar of the court on either side of the gate, and so the posts and buildings laid on those posts joined on each side of this gate.

Verse 15

15 And from the face of the gate of the entrance unto the face of the porch of the inner gate were fifty cubits.

And — This verse seems to sum up all the dimensions; this gate, its porch, and thickness of its walls, and so sum the cubits, six in the thickness of the outer wall, eighteen in the three chambers, twenty in the spaces between the chambers, and six cubits in the thickness in the inner wall of the porch.

Verse 16

16 And there were narrow windows to the little chambers, and to their posts within the gate round about, and likewise to the arches: and windows were round about inward: and upon each post were palm trees.

Narrow windows — Windows narrowed inward to the middle.

Their posts — The upper lintel of each door over which was a window.

To the arches — Windows under the arches between post and post, to give light to the five cubits space between chamber and chamber.

Round about — These were on both sides of the porch within the gate, exactly alike.

Verse 17

17 Then brought he me into the outward court, and, lo, there were chambers, and a pavement made for the court round about: thirty chambers were upon the pavement.

The outward court — So called in regard of the more inward court, between that where he was, and the temple itself; this court, was the second about the temple.

Chambers — Not only lodging rooms for the priests, but also store-houses for tithes and offerings.

A pavement — A beautiful floor laid with checker works. The whole floor of this court was thus paved.

Thirty chambers — That is, fifteen on the south side of the gate, and fifteen on the north side, built over the pavement.

Verse 18

18 And the pavement by the side of the gates over against the length of the gates was the lower pavement.

The pavement — That mentioned, verse 17.

By the side — That part which lay on each side of the gate, and from thence spread itself toward the chambers, leaving a space of pavement of equal breadth with the porch, or gate in the middle.

The length — The length was measured fifty cubits.

The inner pavement — The side pavement was laid somewhat lower than this middle pavement, not only for state, but for the more convenient, keeping it clean; so the middle pavement rose with a little convex surface.

Verse 19

19 Then he measured the breadth from the forefront of the lower gate unto the forefront of the inner court without, an hundred cubits eastward and northward.

The breadth — Of the whole ground between the inner front of one gate and porch, to the outer front of the next gate more inward to the temple.

The lower gate — Called so in respect to the next gate, which was on the higher ground.

The forefront — To the outside front of the gate of the priests court, which was next to this gate now measured, that is from the west front of the lower to the east front of the upper gate.

The inner court — This court from the west front of the lower gate, was one hundred cubits in length to the east front of the gate of the inner court.

East-ward and north-ward — And so was the space from the south front of the court to the north front. So the court was exactly square. Divers courts are here spoken of, which may put us in mind, of the diversity of gifts, graces and offices in the church: as also of the several degrees of glory in the courts and mansions of heaven.

Verse 22

22 And their windows, and their arches, and their palm trees, were after the measure of the gate that looketh toward the east; and they went up unto it by seven steps; and the arches thereof were before them.

Before them — Within the steps or gate.

Verse 23

23 And the gate of the inner court was over against the gate toward the north, and toward the east; and he measured from gate to gate an hundred cubits.

Toward the east — The east gate of the inner court was directly over against the east gate of the outer court, and equally distant from each other.

Verse 26

26 And there were seven steps to go up to it, and the arches thereof were before them: and it had palm trees, one on this side, and another on that side, upon the posts thereof.

To it — The floor, or square court.

Verse 28

28 And he brought me to the inner court by the south gate: and he measured the south gate according to these measures;

Brought me — From the south-gate of the outer court through the porch, and over the hundred cubit pavement, to the south-gate of the inner court.

Verse 32

32 And he brought me into the inner court toward the east: and he measured the gate according to these measures.

The inner court — The court of the priests, which was next to the temple.

Verse 43

43 And within were hooks, an hand broad, fastened round about: and upon the tables was the flesh of the offering.

Within — Within the porch, where these tables stood.

Hooks — Hooks on which the slaughtered sacrifice might be hanged, while they prepared it farther.

Fastened — To walls no doubt, near these tables.

Verse 45

45 And he said unto me, This chamber, whose prospect is toward the south, is for the priests, the keepers of the charge of the house.

The keepers — While, according to their courses, they had the charge of the house of God, and attended on the service of it.

Verse 46

46 And the chamber whose prospect is toward the north is for the priests, the keepers of the charge of the altar: these are the sons of Zadok among the sons of Levi, which come near to the LORD to minister unto him.

The keepers — To preserve the fire perpetually on the altar.

Verse 48

48 And he brought me to the porch of the house, and measured each post of the porch, five cubits on this side, and five cubits on that side: and the breadth of the gate was three cubits on this side, and three cubits on that side.

The breadth — The whole breadth was eleven cubits, but the breadth of each leaf of this folding-gate was three cubits, and they met, or shut on an upright post, set in the middle of the gate space, and this was one cubit broad. And each leaf hung on posts two cubits thick, which amount to eleven cubits.

Chapter Forty-One

The dimensions of the house and various parts of it, ver. 1 - 13.
An account of another building, ver. 14, 15.
The manner of the building of the house, ver. 16, 17.
The ornaments of the house, ver. 18 - 20.
The altar of incense and the table, ver. 21, 22.
The doors between the temple and the oracle, ver. 23 - 26.

Verse 1

1 Afterward he brought me to the temple, and measured the posts, six cubits broad on the one side, and six cubits broad on the other side, which was the breadth of the tabernacle.

The breadth — These walls in their thickness took up as much space as the whole breadth of Moses's tabernacle, Exodus 26:16,22.

Verse 3

3 Then went he inward, and measured the post of the door, two cubits; and the door, six cubits; and the breadth of the door, seven cubits.

Went he — From the porch thro' the body of the temple, to the partition between the body of the temple and the holy of holies.

Measured — Either the thickness of that partition wall, or of the pilasters, which stood one on the one side, and the other on the other side of the door.

Of the door — Or entrance out of the temple into the oracle.

And the door — This door was six cubits broad, and an upright bar or post on which the leaves met, and which was of one cubit's breadth, make out seven cubits.

Verse 4

4 So he measured the length thereof, twenty cubits; and the breadth, twenty cubits, before the temple: and he said unto me, This is the most holy place.

Thereof — Of the holy of holies, which was an exact square.

Before — Parallel with the breadth of the temple.

Verse 5

5 After he measured the wall of the house, six cubits; and the breadth of every side chamber, four cubits, round about the house on every side.

After — Having left the holy of holies, now he is come to take the measures of the outer wall.

The house — The temple.

Six cubits — Three yards thick was this wall from the ground to the first story of the side-chambers.

Side-chamber — Of the lowest floor; for there were three stories of these, and they differed in their breadth, as the wall of the temple, on which they rested, abated of its thickness; for the middle chambers were broader than the lowest by a cubit, and the highest as much broader than the middle.

Round about — On the north, south, and west parts, on each side of every one of these three gates.

Verse 6

6 And the side chambers were three, one over another, and thirty in order; and they entered into the wall which was of the house for the side chambers round about, that they might have hold, but they had not hold in the wall of the house.

They might — That the beams of the chambers might have good and firm resting-hold.

Had not hold — The ends of the beams were not thrust into the main body of the wall of the temple.

Verse 7

7 And there was an enlarging, and a winding about still upward to the side chambers: for the winding about of the house went still upward round about the house: therefore the breadth of the house was still upward, and so increased from the lowest chamber to the highest by the midst.

An enlarging — Of the side chambers, so much of breadth added to the chamber, as was taken from the thickness of the wall; that is, two cubits in the uppermost, and one cubit in the middle-most, more than in the lowest chambers.

A winding about — Winding stairs, which enlarged as the rooms did, and these run up between each two chambers from the bottom to the top; so there were two doors at the head of each pair of stairs, one door opening into one chamber, and the other into the opposite chamber.

For the winding about — These stairs, as they rose in height, enlarged themselves too.

Round about — On all sides of the house where these chambers were.

The breadth — Of each chamber.

Increased — Grew broader by one cubit in every upper chamber. From five in the lowest to six in the middle, and to seven in the highest chamber.

Verse 8

8 I saw also the height of the house round about: the foundations of the side chambers were a full reed of six great cubits.

The foundations — The lowest chamber had properly a foundation laid on the earth, but the floor of the middle, and highest story must be accounted here a foundation; so from the ground to the ceiling of the first room, was six great cubits; from the first to the second, six great cubits; and from the third floor to the roof of the chamber, a like number; to which add we one cubit for thickness of each of the three floors, you have twenty-one cubits for height, ten yards and a half high.

Verse 9

9 The thickness of the wall, which was for the side chamber without, was five cubits: and that which was left was the place of the side chambers that were within.

The place — The walk and wall.

Verse 11

11 And the doors of the side chambers were toward the place that was left, one door toward the north, and another door toward the south: and the breadth of the place that was left was five cubits round about.

The doors — The doors of the lowest row opened into this void paved space.

Verse 12

12 Now the building that was before the separate place at the end toward the west was seventy cubits broad; and the wall of the building was five cubits thick round about, and the length thereof ninety cubits.

The building — This is a new building not yet mentioned, but now measured by itself.

Verse 13

13 So he measured the house, an hundred cubits long; and the separate place, and the building, with the walls thereof, an hundred cubits long;

The house — The whole temple, oracle, sanctuary and porch, with the walls.

The building — On both the north and south-side of the temple.

Verse 14

14 Also the breadth of the face of the house, and of the separate place toward the east, an hundred cubits.

The breadth — The whole front of the house eastward.

Verse 18

18 And it was made with cherubims and palm trees, so that a palm tree was between a cherub and a cherub; and every cherub had two faces;

Cherubim — Generally taken for the portrait of angels, or young men with wings: yet is the description of them very different in different places; in

Ezekiel's vision, Ezekiel 1:5-14; 10:14, Isaiah's vision, Isaiah 6:2, John's vision, Revelation 4:6-8, and in Solomon's temple, 1 Kings 6:23-26.

Verse 19

19 So that the face of a man was toward the palm tree on the one side, and the face of a young lion toward the palm tree on the other side: it was made through all the house round about.

Through all the house — And thus it was through the whole house round about.

Verse 21

21 The posts of the temple were squared, and the face of the sanctuary; the appearance of the one as the appearance of the other.

The face — The door or gate of the temple was square, not arched.

As the appearance — As was the form of the gate of the temple in its larger, so was the form of the gate of the oracle in its lesser dimensions.

Verse 22

22 The altar of wood was three cubits high, and the length thereof two cubits; and the corners thereof, and the length thereof, and the walls thereof, were of wood: and he said unto me, This is the table that is before the LORD.

The altar — Of incense.

The corners — The horns framed out of the four posts at each angle on the top of the altar.

The walls — The sides.

Before the Lord — In the temple, not in the holy of holies.

Verse 23

23 And the temple and the sanctuary had two doors.

Two doors — Each had one.

Verse 25

25 And there were made on them, on the doors of the temple, cherubims and palm trees, like as were made upon the walls; and there were thick planks upon the face of the porch without.

Them — The doors of both temple and oracle.

The temple — Including the holy of holies also.

Chapter Forty-Two

A description of the chambers that were about the courts, ver. 1 - 12. The uses of them, ver. 13 - 14. The whole compass of ground, which was taken up by the house and courts, ver. 15 - 20.

Verse 2

2 Before the length of an hundred cubits was the north door, and the breadth was fifty cubits.

The length — The temple of one hundred cubits long, and of fifty broad, was on the south prospect of these chambers.

Verse 3

3 Over against the twenty cubits which were for the inner court, and over against the pavement which was for the utter court, was gallery against gallery in three stories.

Against gallery — That is, a gallery on the south part toward the inner court, and a gallery toward the pavement north-ward, and between the backs of these galleries were chambers.

Verse 4

4 And before the chambers was a walk of ten cubits breadth inward, a way of one cubit; and their doors toward the north.

A way — Before the galleries probably, was a ledge of one cubit broad, running the whole length from east to west, called here a way, though not designed for any to walk on it.

Verse 5

5 Now the upper chambers were shorter: for the galleries were higher than these, than the lower, and than the middlemost of the building.

Shorter — At first view it should seem to refer to the length, but indeed it refers to the height of the chambers, of which the lowest chamber was highest, the second lower pitched than the first, yet of greater height than the uppermost between the floor and ceiling.

Verse 6

6 For they were in three stories, but had not pillars as the pillars of the courts: therefore the building was straitened more than the lowest and the middlemost from the ground.

As the pillars — So thick and strong as those were.

Verse 7

7 And the wall that was without over against the chambers, toward the utter court on the forepart of the chambers, the length thereof was fifty cubits.

The wall — A wall at a distance from them, perhaps some wall that might keep up a terrace-walk.

Verse 11

11 And the way before them was like the appearance of the chambers which were toward the north, as long as they, and as broad as they: and all their goings out were both according to their fashions, and according to their doors.

The way — The walk.

Was like — Exactly uniform with the fabrick on the north-side.

All their goings — Every window and door.

Were — Framed in the same manner. In all things exactly alike.

Verse 13

13 Then said he unto me, The north chambers and the south chambers, which are before the separate place, they be holy chambers, where the priests that approach unto the LORD shall eat the most holy things: there shall they lay the most holy things, and the meat offering, and the sin offering, and the trespass offering; for the place is holy.

Shall they lay — In some of these chambers the holy things that might be eat, were laid up as in a store-house; and those which were not for present use, were reserved, 'till they were to be used.

Verse 14

14 When the priests enter therein, then shall they not go out of the holy place into the utter court, but there they shall lay their garments wherein they minister; for they are holy; and shall put on other garments, and shall approach to those things which are for the people.

Which are — Which common people may meddle with.

Verse 20

20 He measured it by the four sides: it had a wall round about, five hundred reeds long, and five hundred broad, to make a separation between the sanctuary and the profane place.

Five hundred broad — Each reed was above three yards and an half, so that it was about eight miles round. Thus large were the suburbs of this mystical temple, signifying the great extent of the church in gospel times. It is in part fulfilled already, by the accession of the Gentiles to the church: and will be throughly accomplished, when the fulness of the Gentiles shall come in, and all Israel shall be saved.

A separation — To distinguish, and accordingly to exclude, or admit persons, for all might not go in.

Chapter Forty-Three

In this chapter and the next, the temple - service is described, but under the type of the Old Testament service. The glory of God first fills the temple, ver. 1 - 6.
A promise of God's continuing with his people, if they obey him, ver. 7 - 12.
A description of the altar of burnt offerings, ver. 13 - 17.
Directions for the consecration of that altar, ver. 18 - 27.

Verse 2

2 And, behold, the glory of the God of Israel came from the way of the east: and his voice was like a noise of many waters: and the earth shined with his glory.

Came — When the glory departed, it went eastward, and now it returns, it comes from the east.

And his voice — Though by the voice of God, thunder is sometimes meant, yet here it was an articulate voice.

Verse 3

3 And it was according to the appearance of the vision which I saw, even according to the vision that I saw when I came to destroy the city: and the visions were like the vision that I saw by the river Chebar; and I fell upon my face.

And it — This glory of the God of Israel.

To destroy — To declare, that their sins would ruin their city, chap. 9:3,4.

I fell — Overwhelmed, and as it were swallowed up.

Verse 4

4 And the glory of the LORD came into the house by the way of the gate whose prospect is toward the east.

Came — The sins of Israel caused the glory of the Lord to go out of his house, now the repentance of Israel is blest with the return of this glory.

Verse 6

6 And I heard him speaking unto me out of the house; and the man stood by me.

The man — Christ.

Stood — To encourage, and strengthen him.

Verse 7

7 And he said unto me, Son of man, the place of my throne, and the place of the soles of my feet, where I will dwell in the midst of the children of Israel for ever, and my holy name, shall the house of Israel no more defile, neither they, nor their kings, by their whoredom, nor by the carcases of their kings in their high places.

He — The glorious God of Israel.

My throne — The throne of his grace is in his temple; in the dispensations of grace, God manifests himself a king.

My feet — Speaking after the manner of men, and expressing his abode and rest, in his temple, as the type, in his church, as the antitype.

In their high places — Perhaps some kings were buried in the temples of their idols, near the idols they worshipped.

Verse 8

8 In their setting of their threshold by my thresholds, and their post by my posts, and the wall between me and them, they have even defiled my holy name by their abominations that they have committed: wherefore I have consumed them in mine anger.

Their threshold — The kings of Judah and Israel, built temples and altars for their idols, and these are called their thresholds. They erected these in the courts, or near the courts of the temple.

Abominations — Idolatries, and wickednesses not to be named.

Verse 9

9 Now let them put away their whoredom, and the carcases of their kings, far from me, and I will dwell in the midst of them for ever.

Far from me — From my temple.

Verse 10

10 Thou son of man, shew the house to the house of Israel, that they may be ashamed of their iniquities: and let them measure the pattern.

Son of man — Ezekiel, who is called thus above eighty times in this book.

Shew — Describe it to them in all the parts.

To the house — To the rulers, prophets, and priests especially, not excluding others.

Their iniquities — When they shall blush to see what glory their iniquities had ruined.

Verse 12

12 This is the law of the house; Upon the top of the mountain the whole limit thereof round about shall be most holy. Behold, this is the law of the house.

The law — This is the first comprehensive rule: holiness becomes God's house; and this relative holiness referred to personal and real holiness.

The top — The whole circuit of this mountain shall be holy, but the top of it on which the temple stands, shall be most holy.

Verse 13

13 And these are the measures of the altar after the cubits: The cubit is a cubit and an hand breadth; even the bottom shall be a cubit, and the breadth a cubit, and the border thereof by the edge thereof round about shall be a span: and this shall be the higher place of the altar.

The altar — Of burnt-offerings.

And an hand-breath — The sacred cubit, three inches longer than the common cubit.

The bottom — The ledge or settle, fastened to the altar on all sides at the bottom, shall be a cubit in height.

The breadth — From the edge of this bench on the outside to the edge where it joined the body of the altar, a cubit, and this the breadth, twenty one inches, broad enough for the priests to walk on.

Border — A ledge going round on all the squares.

The edge — On the outer edge of this settle a span high.

The back — As the back bears burdens, so this was to bear the weight of the whole altar.

Verse 14

14 And from the bottom upon the ground even to the lower settle shall be two cubits, and the breadth one cubit; and from the lesser settle even to the greater settle shall be four cubits, and the breadth one cubit.

From the bottom — From the first ledge, which was a cubit broad, and a cubit high from the ground.

To the lower — To the top of that square settle, which is called lower, because another settle is raised upon it.

Two cubits — In height.

The lesser — From the highest edge of the uppermost settle, down to the cubit broad ledge about the lower settle.

The greater — So called, because it exceeded the upper settle a cubit in breadth.

Four cubits — In height.

Verse 15

15 So the altar shall be four cubits; and from the altar and upward shall be four horns.

Four cubits — In height.

From the altar — From the top of the altar.

Verse 17

17 And the settle shall be fourteen cubits long and fourteen broad in the four squares thereof; and the border about it shall be half a cubit; and the bottom thereof shall be a cubit about; and his stairs shall look toward the east.

Stairs — Or steps, for such they needed, (probably each stair about one fourth of a cubit,) to carry them, up to the first and second settles.

Verse 19

19 And thou shalt give to the priests the Levites that be of the seed of Zadok, which approach unto me, to minister unto me, saith the Lord GOD, a young bullock for a sin offering.

Give — Direct, or command that it be given.

Verse 20

20 And thou shalt take of the blood thereof, and put it on the four horns of it, and on the four corners of the settle, and upon the border round about: thus shalt thou cleanse and purge it.

Shalt take — Appoint it to be taken.

Verse 21

21 Thou shalt take the bullock also of the sin offering, and he shall burn it in the appointed place of the house, without the sanctuary.

He — The priest.

In the appointed place — That is, in the court of the house, and on the altar appointed; this is the first day's sacrifice.

Verse 22

22 And on the second day thou shalt offer a kid of the goats without blemish for a sin offering; and they shall cleanse the altar, as they did cleanse it with the bullock.

They — The priests in attendance.

Verse 23

23 When thou hast made an end of cleansing it, thou shalt offer a young bullock without blemish, and a ram out of the flock without blemish.

Shalt offer — On the third day, and so on, through seven days.

Verse 24

24 And thou shalt offer them before the LORD, and the priests shall cast salt upon them, and they shall offer them up for a burnt offering unto the LORD.

Shalt offer — Direct them to offer.

Salt — It may allude to the perpetuity of the covenant thus made by sacrifice.

Verse 26

26 Seven days shall they purge the altar and purify it; and they shall consecrate themselves.

They — The priests in course.

Verse 27

27 And when these days are expired, it shall be, that upon the eighth day, and so forward, the priests shall make your burnt offerings upon the altar, and your peace offerings; and I will accept you, saith the Lord GOD.

I will accept you — Those that give themselves to God, shall be accepted of God, their persons first, and then their performances, through the mediator.

Chapter Forty-Four

The appropriating the east-gate of the temple to the prince, ver. 1 - 3.
A reproof to Israel for their former profanations of the sanctuary, and a caution, ver. 4 - 9.
The degrading of one part of the Levites, and establishing of the family of Zadock in the priesthood, ver. 10 - 16.

Laws and ordinances concerning the priesthood, ver. 17 - 31.

Verse 2

2 Then said the LORD unto me; This gate shall be shut, it shall not be opened, and no man shall enter in by it; because the LORD, the God of Israel, hath entered in by it, therefore it shall be shut.

Shall not be opened — Shall not ordinarily stand open.

No man — None of the common people.

The Lord — That glory which was the visible sign of his presence.

Verse 3

3 It is for the prince; the prince, he shall sit in it to eat bread before the LORD; he shall enter by the way of the porch of that gate, and shall go out by the way of the same.

He — The king might sit before the Lord, others might not.

Bread — That part of the sacrifice, which was allowed to the offerer.

Verse 4

4 Then brought he me the way of the north gate before the house: and I looked, and, behold, the glory of the LORD filled the house of the LORD: and I fell upon my face.

He — Christ in the appearance of a man.

Verse 5

5 And the LORD said unto me, Son of man, mark well, and behold with thine eyes, and hear with thine ears all that I say unto thee concerning all the ordinances of the house of the LORD, and all the laws thereof; and mark well the entering in of the house, with every going forth of the sanctuary.

The entering — The persons who may, and who may not enter.

The sanctuary — Taken here for the courts, rather than the house itself.

Verse 6

6 And thou shalt say to the rebellious, even to the house of Israel, Thus saith the Lord GOD; O ye house of Israel, let it suffice you of all your abominations,

Let it suffice — Let the time you have spent on your sins suffice.

Verse 7

7 In that ye have brought into my sanctuary strangers, uncircumcised in heart, and uncircumcised in flesh, to be in my sanctuary, to pollute it, even my house, when ye offer my bread, the fat and the blood, and they have broken my covenant because of all your abominations.

Bread — Either the meal-offering or first-fruits of corn and dough, and the shew-bread.

They — The whole nation of the Jews.

Verse 8

8 And ye have not kept the charge of mine holy things: but ye have set keepers of my charge in my sanctuary for yourselves.

Have not kept — You have not observed the laws I gave you for the keeping of my holy things, house, sacrifices, and worship.

Have set — You have substituted others in your rooms.

Verse 10

10 And the Levites that are gone away far from me, when Israel went astray, which went astray away from me after their idols; they shall even bear their iniquity.

Are gone away — By their idolatry.

Verse 11

11 Yet they shall be ministers in my sanctuary, having charge at the gates of the house, and ministering to the house: they shall slay the burnt offering and the sacrifice for the people, and they shall stand before them to minister unto them.

Ministers — Servants employed in the lowest work.

Sanctuary — Not the temple itself, but about the courts of it.

Having charge — They shall be porters to open and shut, and sweep, and go on errands.

To minister — To wait on the priests.

Verse 12

12 Because they ministered unto them before their idols, and caused the house of Israel to fall into iniquity; therefore have I lifted up mine hand against them, saith the Lord GOD, and they shall bear their iniquity.

Iniquity — The punishment of it.

Verse 13

13 And they shall not come near unto me, to do the office of a priest unto me, nor to come near to any of my holy things, in the most holy place: but they shall bear their shame, and their abominations which they have committed.

Shall bear their shame — They shall be dealt with according to their abominations, and bear the punishment thereof.

Verse 15

15 But the priests the Levites, the sons of Zadok, that kept the charge of my sanctuary when the children of Israel went astray from me, they shall come near to me to minister unto me, and they shall stand before me to offer unto me the fat and the blood, saith the Lord GOD:

That kept the charge — Were constant, zealous, and faithful in their priestly office.

Verse 16

16 They shall enter into my sanctuary, and they shall come near to my table, to minister unto me, and they shall keep my charge.

Into my sanctuary — Both to the altar, to the temple, and the high-priest into the holy of holies.

Come near — To set the shew-bread on, and to take it off.

To minister — To offer sacrifice at the altar, and incense in the house. God will put marks of honour upon those who are faithful to him in trying times, and will, employ those in his service, who have kept close to it, when others drew back.

Verse 17

17 And it shall come to pass, that when they enter in at the gates of the inner court, they shall be clothed with linen garments; and no wool shall come upon them, whiles they minister in the gates of the inner court, and within.

And within — In the temple.

Verse 19

19 And when they go forth into the utter court, even into the utter court to the people, they shall put off their garments wherein they ministered, and lay them in the holy chambers, and they shall put on other garments; and they shall not sanctify the people with their garments.

Shall not sanctify — By the law, common things, touching holy things, became consecrated, and no more fit for common use.

Verse 20

20 Neither shall they shave their heads, nor suffer their locks to grow long; they shall only poll their heads.

To grow long — Priding themselves in it, as Absalom.

Shall only poll — When the hair is grown, they shall cut the ends of their hair, and keep it in moderate size.

Verse 21

21 Neither shall any priest drink wine, when they enter into the inner court.

Drink wine — Or any other strong liquor, when they go either to trim the lamps or set the shew-bread in order, or to offer incense in the temple, or when they go to the altar to offer a sacrifice, which stood in the inner court.

Verse 24

24 And in controversy they shall stand in judgment; and they shall judge it according to my judgments: and they shall keep my laws and my statutes in all mine assemblies; and they shall hallow my sabbaths.

Shall judge — Shall determine the controversy.

Assemblies — Publick congregations.

Verse 26

26 And after he is cleansed, they shall reckon unto him seven days.

Cleansed — After for seven days he hath kept from the dead.

They — The priests, who are about the house of God, shall appoint seven days more to this defiled person for his cleansing before he is admitted into the sanctuary.

Verse 28

28 And it shall be unto them for an inheritance: I am their inheritance: and ye shall give them no possession in Israel: I am their possession.

It — The sin-offering: but under this one, all other offerings are couched.

For an inheritance — Instead of lands and cities.

Verse 30

30 And the first of all the firstfruits of all things, and every oblation of all, of every sort of your oblations, shall be the priest's: ye shall also give unto the priest the first of your dough, that he may cause the blessing to rest in thine house.

And the first — So soon as the first-fruits are ripe in the field, your vineyards, and olive yards.

Every oblation — Whether free-will offering, or prescribed.

The first of your dough — 'Tis conceived this was of every mass of dough they made, and of the first of the dough, which every year they first made of the new corn, as by the custom of the Jews at this day appears.

That he — The priest may bless, and pray for thee.

Chapter Forty-Five

The division of the holy land, ver. 1 - 8. The ordinances that were given both to the prince and to the people, ver. 9 - 12. The oblations to be offered, and the princes part therein, ver. 13 - 17. Particularly, in the beginning of the year, ver. 18 - 20.
And in the passover, and feast of tabernacles, ver. 21 - 25.

Verse 2

2 Of this there shall be for the sanctuary five hundred in length, with five hundred in breadth, square round about; and fifty cubits round about for the suburbs thereof.

Of this — Whole portion of twenty five thousand cubits long, or twelve miles and half, and ten thousand broad, or five miles and a little more.

For the sanctuary — For a platform for the sanctuary, both house and court.

Verse 3

3 And of this measure shalt thou measure the length of five and twenty thousand, and the breadth of ten thousand: and in it shall be the sanctuary and the most holy place.

And in it — In the center of this.

Verse 6

6 And ye shall appoint the possession of the city five thousand broad, and five and twenty thousand long, over against the oblation of the holy portion: it shall be for the whole house of Israel.

The possession — Land to be a possession to the citizens of Jerusalem, and to be the content of the city.

Broad — About two miles and half broad, and twelve miles and half long.

Long — This must run along parallel in length with the holy portion, though but half its breadth.

For the whole house — As the capital city, to which the tribe's resort, it must be large enough to entertain them.

Verse 7

7 And a portion shall be for the prince on the one side and on the other side of the oblation of the holy portion, and of the possession of the city, before the oblation of the holy portion, and before the possession of the city, from the west side westward, and from the east side eastward: and the length shall be over against one of the portions, from the west border unto the east border.

The prince — The king.

Our side — One half of the prince's

portion lay on the west side of those three already set out.

The other side — The other half lay on the east-side thereof, so the portion of the city, Levites and priests, lay in the middle.

The holy portion — Of priests, and Levites, and sanctuary.

Before — It lay parallel as broad as these three were broad, and so run on both sides in its breadth from north to south, and had its length as the other, from east to west.

Over against — What is called now over-against, or by the side, is called before three times together. So now you have an exact square of twenty-five thousand cubits laid out for God, the Levites and city, which appears thus in the breadth. 10000 For the priests. 10000 For the Levites. 5000 For the city. And the length of each, twenty-five thousand, that is twelve miles and half square.

Verse 9

9 Thus saith the Lord GOD; Let it suffice you, O princes of Israel: remove violence and spoil, and execute judgment and justice, take away your exactions from my people, saith the Lord GOD.

Let it suffice — Be content, aim not at more.

Verse 11

11 The ephah and the bath shall be of one measure, that the bath may contain the tenth part of an homer, and the ephah the tenth part of an homer: the measure thereof shall be after the homer.

Of one measure — One shall contain as much as the other, the ephah shall contain as many gallons of dry, as the bath of liquid things.

An homer — Thirty bushels. So the ephah will be three bushels in dry things, and the bath eight gallons in liquid things.

Verse 12

12 And the shekel shall be twenty gerahs: twenty shekels, five and twenty shekels, fifteen shekels, shall be your maneh.

Twenty gerahs — A gerah was one penny half-penny, the shekel then was two shillings and six-pence, twenty shekels was two pounds ten shillings, fifteen shekels was one pound seventeen shillings and six-pence, and twenty five was three pound two shillings and six-pence.

Maneh — It seems there was the small, the middle, and the great Maneh.

Verse 13

13 This is the oblation that ye shall offer; the sixth part of an ephah of an homer of wheat, and ye shall give the sixth part of an ephah of an homer of barley:

Offer — In the daily service, the morning and evening sacrifice.

Verse 14

14 Concerning the ordinance of oil, the bath of oil, ye shall offer the tenth part of a bath out of the cor, which is an homer of ten baths; for ten baths are an homer:

Bath — Which contained about twenty-four gallons.

The cor — Or homer; these were two names of the same measure.

Verse 16

16 All the people of the land shall give this oblation for the prince in Israel.

With the prince — By a common purse of prince and people.

Verse 18

18 Thus saith the Lord GOD; In the first month, in the first day of the month, thou shalt take a young bullock without blemish, and cleanse the sanctuary:

Thou shalt take — Procure, this the prince must do.

Verse 20

20 And so thou shalt do the seventh day of the month for every one that erreth, and for him that is simple: so shall ye reconcile the house.

For every one that erreth — For all the errors of all the house of Israel, through ignorance.

For him that is simple — That is half-witted, or a fool.

Reconcile — Cleanse, as verse 18, which legally was defiled by those errors done in the city, or courts of the house, whither these persons might come.

Verse 21

21 In the first month, in the fourteenth day of the month, ye shall have the passover, a feast of seven days; unleavened bread shall be eaten.

In the first month — Nisan, which is part of March, and part of April with us.

Verse 22

22 And upon that day shall the prince prepare for himself and for all the people of the land a bullock for a sin offering.

Upon that day — Upon the fourteenth day, on which the passover was slain.

Verse 24

24 And he shall prepare a meat offering of an ephah for a bullock, and an ephah for a ram, and an hin of oil for an ephah.

An hin — This was about one gallon and three quarters of a pint.

Verse 25

25 In the seventh month, in the fifteenth day of the month, shall he do the like in the feast of the seven days, according to the sin offering, according to the burnt offering, and according to the meat offering, and according to the oil.

In the seventh month — According to their ecclesiastical account, which is Tisri, and answers to part of our August and September.

In the fifteenth day — On that day the feast of tabernacles began, and continued seven days.

He — The prince.

In the feast of the seven days — Hence we also may learn the necessity of frequently repeating the same religious exercises. Indeed the sacrifice of atonement was offered once for all. But the sacrifice of acknowledgement, that of a broken heart, that of a thankful heart, must be offered every day. And these spiritual sacrifices are always acceptable to God through Christ Jesus.

Chapter Forty-Six

Farther rules for the worship of the priests and the people, ver. 1 - 15.
A rule, for the prince's disposal of his inheritance, ver. 16 - 18.
A description of the places for the boiling and baking the offerings, ver. 19 - 24.

Verse 3

3 Likewise the people of the land shall worship at the door of this gate before the LORD in the sabbaths and in the new moons.

In the sabbaths — Both weekly and other holy days, which are called sabbaths.

Verse 9

9 But when the people of the land shall come before the LORD in the solemn feasts, he that entereth in by the way of the north gate to worship shall go out by the way of the south gate; and he that entereth by the way of the south gate shall go forth by the way of the north gate: he shall not return by the way of the gate whereby he came in, but shall go forth over against it.

Go forth over against it — Perhaps, only to prevent all jostling and confusion.

Verse 17

17 But if he give a gift of his inheritance to one of his servants, then it shall be his to the year of liberty; after it shall return to the prince: but his inheritance shall be his sons' for them.

His inheritance — Whatever lands of the prince are given to servants, shall at the year of Jubilee revert to the sons of the prince.

For them — And to theirs after them.

Verse 20

20 Then said he unto me, This is the place where the priests shall boil the trespass offering and the sin offering, where they shall bake the meat offering; that they bear them not out into the utter court, to sanctify the people.

The outer court — Where the people were.

Verse 21

21 Then he brought me forth into the utter court, and caused me to pass by the four corners of the court; and, behold, in every corner of the court there was a court.

A court — A smaller court made up on the outer sides with the walls of the greater square, and on the inside made with two walls, the one forty cubits long, the other thirty cubits broad.

Verse 23

23 And there was a row of building round about in them, round about them four, and it was made with boiling places under the rows round about.

A row of building — A range of building on the inside of the walls of the lesser courts.

Four — Four courts in the four corners.

Chapter Forty-Seven

The vision of the holy waters, ver. 1 - 12.
The borders of the land of Canaan, ver. 13 - 23.

Verse 1

1 Afterward he brought me again unto the door of the house; and, behold, waters issued out from under the threshold of the house eastward: for the forefront of the house stood toward the east, and the waters came down from under from the right side of the house, at the south side of the altar.

Eastward — The fountain lay to the west, the conduit pipes were laid to bring the water to the temple, and so must run eastward, and perhaps one main pipe might be laid under the east-gate of the temple.

The right side — On the south-side of the temple.

Verse 2

2 Then brought he me out of the way of the gate northward, and led me about the way without unto the utter gate by the way that looketh eastward; and, behold, there ran out waters on the right side.

Out — Of the inmost court.

The outer gate — The outmost north-gate in the wall that compassed the whole mountain of the Lord's house.

Verse 3

3 And when the man that had the line in his hand went forth eastward, he measured a thousand cubits, and he brought me through the waters; the waters were to the ankles.

He measured — By the line in his hand.

He brought me — Went before, and the prophet followed; all this was in vision.

Verse 8

8 Then said he unto me, These waters issue out toward the east country, and go down into the desert, and go into the sea: which being brought forth into the sea, the waters shall be healed.

The sea — The Dead-sea, or lake of Sodom.

Shall be healed — The waters of the sea shall be healed, made wholesome. So where the grace of God from his temple and altar flows, it heals the corrupt nature of man, and renders barren terrible deserts, as a land of waters and gardens.

Verse 9

9 And it shall come to pass, that every thing that liveth, which moveth, whithersoever the rivers shall come, shall live: and there shall be a very great multitude of fish, because these waters shall come thither: for they shall be healed; and every thing shall live whither the river cometh.

Shall live — Be preserved alive, and thrive, whereas no fish can live in the Dead-sea.

For they — The poisonous waters of the Dead-sea shall be made wholesome for fish.

Shall live — Thrive, and multiply in the virtue of the healing streams. Thus is the fruitfulness of the grace of God in the church set forth.

Verse 10

10 And it shall come to pass, that the fishers shall stand upon it from Engedi even unto Eneglaim; they shall be a place to spread forth nets; their fish shall be according to their kinds, as the fish of the great sea, exceeding many.

En-gedi — Which lay on the south-west of the lake of Sodom.

En-eglaim — A city on the north-east of the Dead-sea.

To spread forth nets — All along on the west-side of this sea to dry them.

Verse 12

12 And by the river upon the bank thereof, on this side and on that side, shall grow all trees for meat, whose leaf shall not fade, neither shall the fruit thereof be consumed: it shall bring forth new fruit according to his months, because their waters they issued out of the sanctuary: and the fruit thereof shall be for meat, and the leaf thereof for medicine.

Consumed — Never be consumed, never decay, there shall always be fruit, and enough.

Their waters — Those that watered them.

Issued out — And so carried a blessing with them.

Verse 13

13 Thus saith the Lord GOD; This shall be the border, whereby ye shall inherit the land according to the twelve tribes of Israel: Joseph shall have two portions.

The border — The utmost bounds of the whole land.

Shall inherit — That is, shall divide for inheritance to the tribes of Israel.

Joseph — That is, the two sons of Joseph, Ephraim, and Manasseh.

Verse 15

15 And this shall be the border of the land toward the north side, from the great sea, the way of Hethlon, as men go to Zedad;

The great sea — The Mediterranean, which was the greatest sea the Jews knew.

Verse 18

18 And the east side ye shall measure from Hauran, and from Damascus, and from Gilead, and from the land of Israel by Jordan, from the border unto the east sea. And this is the east side.

The east sea — The Dead-sea, which lay on the east of Jerusalem. Thus a line drawn from Damascus through Auranitis, Gilead, the land of Israel beyond Jordan to the east-sea, made the eastern frontier.

Verse 19

19 And the south side southward, from Tamar even to the waters of strife in Kadesh, the river to the great sea. And this is the south side southward.

The river — Called the river of Egypt, lay directly in the way to Egypt from Jerusalem.

The great sea — To the south-west part of the Mediterranean sea near Gaza.

Verse 22

22 And it shall come to pass, that ye shall divide it by lot for an inheritance unto you, and to the strangers that sojourn among you, which shall beget children among you: and they shall be unto you as born in the country among the children of Israel; they shall have inheritance with you among the tribes of Israel.

Children — Who from their birth should be invested with this right of inheriting.

Verse 23

23 And it shall come to pass, that in what tribe the stranger sojourneth, there shall ye give him his inheritance, saith the Lord GOD.

His inheritance — This certainly looks at gospel times, when the partition-wall between Jew and Gentile was taken down, and both put on a level before God, both made one in Christ Jesus.

Chapter Forty-Eight

The portion of seven tribes, ver. 1 - 7.
The allotment of land for the sanctuary, priests and Levites, ver. 8 - 14.
For the city and prince, ver. 15 - 22.
For the other five tribes, ver. 23 - 29.
A plan of the city, its gates, and new name, ver. 30 - 35.

Verse 15

15 And the five thousand, that are left in the breadth over against the five and twenty thousand, shall be a profane place for the city, for dwelling, and for suburbs: and the city shall be in the midst thereof.

A profane place — A common, not consecrated place.

Verse 16

16 And these shall be the measures thereof; the north side four thousand and five hundred, and the south side four thousand and five hundred, and on the east side four thousand and five hundred, and the west side four thousand and five hundred.

The measures thereof — The extent and proportions of the city, a square of four thousand five hundred shall be taken out of the middle of the twenty five thousand or the ground-plat of the city. So it shall be an equilateral square, every side exactly the same, north, south, east, and west, four thousand five hundred apiece, by which measures the whole content is visible eighteen thousand cubits not reeds.

Verse 18

18 And the residue in length over against the oblation of the holy portion shall be ten thousand eastward, and ten thousand westward: and it shall be over against the oblation of the holy portion; and the increase thereof shall be for food unto them that serve the city.

For food — For the maintenance of the city-officers.

Verse 20

20 All the oblation shall be five and twenty thousand by five and twenty thousand: ye shall offer the holy oblation foursquare, with the possession of the city.

The possession — The land assigned for the city.

Verse 28

28 And by the border of Gad, at the

south side southward, the border shall be even from Tamar unto the waters of strife in Kadesh, and to the river toward the great sea.

To the river — The river of Egypt.

Verse 35

35 It was round about eighteen thousand measures: and the name of the city from that day shall be, The LORD is there.

Eighteen thousand cubits — About five miles in compass.

From that day — From the day of the Lord's restoring this people, and rebuilding their city, and their thankful, holy, and pure worshipping of God there, from that day it shall be said of Jerusalem.

The Lord is there — The Lord who as his name alone is Jehovah, so is the only true God, faithful to his promise, rich in mercy, glorious in majesty, righteous in his judgments, wise and holy in his government, whose presence makes us happy, whose withdrawing from us leaves us to misery. This God will by his favour and presence, bring the confluence of all good to persons, families, and cities; this God will be there to dwell, govern, defend, prosper, and crown. Such is to be the case of earthly Jerusalem, such shall be for ever the case of the heavenly Jerusalem. Such is the case of every true believer, who may, wherever he is, in his way of duty, still write Jehovah-Shammah, My God is here. And 'tis best to be where he is 'till he bring us within the gates of the glorious city, where inconceivable light and love from the immediate presence of God, give every one an eternal demonstration that God is here: to him be glory for ever.

Printed in Great Britain
by Amazon